Travel Guide To Bilbao 2023

Exploring the Vibrant City: A Comprehensive Travel Guide to Bilbao in 2023

Scott O. Cortes

Copyright ©2023,Scott O. Cortes
All rights reserved. No part of this publication may be reproduced, stored in a retrieval system or transmitted in any form or by any means, electronic, mechanical, photocopying, recording or otherwise without prior written permission of the author, expect in the case of brief quotations embodied in critical reviews and certain other noncommercial uses permitted by copyright law.

Table Of Content

INTRODUCTION
- Welcome to Bilbao
- About This Guide
- Practical Information

GETTING TO KNOW BILBAO
- History of Bilbao
- Geography and Climate
- Local Culture and Customs
- Festivals and Events

PLANNING YOUR TRIP
- Best Time to Visit
- Duration of Stay
- Budgeting and Expenses
- Essential Travel Tips

EXPLORING BILBAO'S NEIGHBOURHOODS
- Old Town (Casco Viejo)

Ensanche
Abando
Indautxu
Deusto
Getxo

TOP ATTRACTIONS IN BILBAO
Guggenheim Museum
Santiago Cathedral
Arriaga Theater
Bilbao Fine Art Museum
Zubizuri Bridge
Alhóndiga Cultural Center

OUTDOOR ADVENTURES AND NATURE
Mount Artxanda
Dona Casilda Park
Urdaibai Biosphere Reserve
Bilbao's Beaches

GASTRONOMY AND NIGHTLIFE
Traditional Basque Cuisine

Pintxos Culture
Best Restaurants and Bars
Nightclubs and Entertainment

SHOPPING IN BILBAO
Shopping Districts
Unique Souvenirs and Crafts

DAY TRIPS FROM BILBAO
San Sebastian
Vitoria-Gasteiz
Rioja Wine Region
Santander

PRACTICAL INFORMATION
Transportation Within Bilbao
Accommodation Options
Local Customs and Etiquette
Safety Tips and Emergency Contacts
Useful Websites and Resources

LANGUAGE GUIDE

Basic Spanish Phrases

CONCLUSION
Fond Farewell to Bilbao

INTRODUCTION

Thank you for visiting "Travel Guide to Bilbao 2023: Exploring the Vibrant City." You may explore Bilbao's rich culture, history, and sights in 2023 with the help of our thorough travel guide.

This book will give you insightful information, useful advice, and must-see suggestions to help you make the most of your trip, whether you're a frequent visitor or a first-timer to this dynamic city.

Northern Spain's Basque Country is home to the city of Bilbao, which is renowned for its distinctive fusion of tradition and modernity. Every traveller will be captivated by Bilbao's beautiful architecture, top-notch museums, mouthwatering cuisine, and breathtaking vistas. We hope to take you on a tour of the city's neighbourhoods, prominent attractions, outdoor activities, delectable cuisine, and day trip hotspots in this guide.

We have provided details on the ideal time to visit, suggested lengths of stay, and spending advice to assist you in making an informed decision about your trip. In order to make your stay seamless and pleasurable, we also offer helpful advice about available modes of transportation, lodging options, and regional customs.

This guide includes thorough descriptions of Bilbao's well-known attractions, including the Guggenheim Museum, Santiago Cathedral, and Zubizuri Bridge, as well as lesser-known undiscovered jewels that highlight the city's distinct appeal. A component of our website is devoted to the city's outdoor pursuits, including hiking options and excursions to lovely parks and beaches.

Without enjoying Bilbao's famed cuisine, a visit would not be complete. We direct you to the top eateries, pubs, and marketplaces where you may sample regional specialties, from authentic Basque food to the thriving pintxos culture. We also provide suggestions for interesting shopping areas and gifts to bring home as keepsakes.

We have a list of day trips to surrounding places including San Sebastián, Vitoria-Gasteiz, and the Rioja Wine Region for individuals who want to venture outside of Bilbao. These locations offer a taste of the larger Basque Country and its varied attractions.

We've included a language guide with fundamental Spanish phrases as well as an extensive appendix with maps, suggested reading, and helpful websites and resources to improve your vacation experience.

So buckle up, prepare for an amazing voyage, and let "Travel Guide to Bilbao 2023" be your dependable guide as you explore this dynamic city's wonders. Let's plunge into Bilbao's heart and make lifelong memories there.

Welcome to Bilbao

Greetings from Bilbao, a bustling city tucked away in the centre of the Basque Country! Bilbao, which is renowned for its extensive history, outstanding architecture, and vibrant environment, provides a special synthesis of tradition and modernity.

You'll be welcomed by this enchanting city's kind and welcoming environment as soon as you arrive. The welcoming residents are always willing to share their passion for Bilbao and lead you to its secret attractions. Prepare to discover the city's many neighbourhoods, savour delectable cuisine, and immerse yourself in its rich cultural history.

Famous landmarks may be found in Bilbao, such as the Guggenheim Museum, where art lovers can view modern masterpieces. You are invited to explore the lovely Casco Viejo, or Old Town, with its winding alleyways, charming shops, and mouthwatering pintxos.

Take a stroll along the Nervion River and be mesmerised by the magnificent buildings that line its banks, including the Euskalduna Palace and the Zubizuri Bridge. With a variety of bars, clubs, and live music venues where you can dance the night away, the city's dynamic nightlife beckons.

Bilbao has something to offer everyone, whether you're a history buff, an art enthusiast, a foodie, or just looking for a once-in-a-lifetime adventure. It is a place worth visiting due to its vibrant energy, diverse events, and stunning scenery.

Welcome to Bilbao, then! Get ready to be enveloped by its warmth, delighted by its charm, and inspired by its ingenuity. As you go off on a fantastic adventure through the city's streets, allow the spirit of the place to engulf you. As you experience each moment, make memories that will last a lifetime.

About This Guide

During your trip to Bilbao, the "Travel Guide to Bilbao 2023: Exploring the Vibrant City" is intended to be your all-inclusive travel companion. What to anticipate from this guide is as follows:

- **Information that is Current:** This manual is based on the most recent data available through 2023. It guarantees that you have access to the most recent information about attractions, lodgings, dining alternatives, transportation, and other topics.

- **Detailed Coverage:** In order to give you comprehensive coverage of Bilbao, we have carefully chosen a wide range of topics. This guide covers everything from the city's history and culture to its major attractions, neighbourhoods, outdoor activities, gastronomy, and day trip ideas.

- You may find helpful hints, insider suggestions, and recommendations all throughout the guide to help you make the most of your time in Bilbao. Our goal is to improve your travel experience, whether it be through suggestions for the ideal time to go, money-saving tricks, or ideas for undiscovered gems.

- Maps and visuals are presented to give a visual picture of Bilbao's geography, attractions, and important sites of interest. Visual aids include maps, photographs, and illustrations. You will be able to easily navigate the city and comprehend the information given thanks to these pictures.

- **Language Guide**: We have provided a simple Spanish language guide to help you communicate with the locals. It includes idioms and expressions that are frequently used and will be useful to you while you are visiting Bilbao.

- **Useful Resources:** This guide's appendix section lists additional resources, including books to read and websites and other information sources, that can help you learn more about Bilbao and the area around it.

This guide is made to suit your requirements and interests, whether you're a solitary traveller, a family on vacation, or a group of friends touring the city. It strives to be your go-to source for learning about the best Bilbao has to offer and making sure you have a fulfilling and memorable trip.

As you go on an exciting tour through its streets, immerse yourself in its culture, and make priceless memories in this wonderful location, immerse yourself in the dynamic city of Bilbao and let this guide be your trustworthy travel companion.

Practical Information

It's important to educate yourself with some useful facts before starting your trip to Bilbao so you can make the most of it. Here are some important facts to think about:

- Best Time to Visit: Although Bilbao has a moderate climate all year round, spring (April to June) and fall (September to October) are the busiest travel seasons. These months provide excellent weather, fewer visitors, and a variety of festivals and cultural activities. Winter (December to February) is colder with sporadic rain, while summer (July to August) can be hot and muggy.

- The best length of your stay in Bilbao will depend on your interests and the activities you have planned. It is advised to spend at least two to three days exploring the city and its top attractions. Consider extending your trip to five or more days if you want to go on day trips or learn more about the local way of life.

- Expenses and budgeting: Bilbao can accommodate a variety of budgets. While the cost of lodging, food, and activities can vary, there are solutions to fit various budgetary constraints. It's a good idea to plan your budget in advance, taking into account expenditures for things like lodging, meals, transportation, admission fees to sites, and any extra activities you might want to do.

- Currency: The Euro (€), like the rest of Spain, is the official unit of exchange in Bilbao. It's a good idea to carry some cash with you for quick transactions and in case you come across any businesses that might not accept cards.

Although many hotels, restaurants, and shops take credit cards, it's usually a good idea to have some cash on hand for convenience.

- Spanish is the official language in Bilbao. Although English is widely used in tourist areas, hotels, and larger enterprises, many people also speak Basque. To make conversation easier while travelling, it can be useful to learn a few fundamental Spanish phrases.

- Transit: It is simple to move around the city and its surroundings because of Bilbao's well-developed transit network, which includes buses, trams, and a metro system. The Bilbao Card, which may be purchased, provides unrestricted access to the public transit system and special attraction discounts. Additionally accessible are taxis, which may be called on the street or reserved via apps.

- Bilbao offers a variety of lodging options to accommodate different tastes and price ranges. You can choose from upscale hotels, inexpensive hostels, and vacation homes to suit your preferences. It's a good idea to reserve your lodging in advance, especially during the busiest travel times.

- Though Bilbao is a relatively safe city, it is still advisable to use caution when travelling. Be cautious with your possessions, especially in busy places, and keep valuables in hotel safes. Having travel insurance that covers medical crises and trip cancellations is also a good idea.

- Local Customs and Etiquette: The inhabitants of Bilbao are renowned for their friendliness and warmth. It is normal to shake hands when you meet someone and to look them in the eye while speaking. Although not required, tipping is recommended when receiving good service. In restaurants, it's customary to round up the amount or leave a 10% tip.

- Emergency Contact Information: The country's main emergency number in Spain is 112. For police, medical, and fire situations, dial this number.

You'll be well-equipped to travel Bilbao with ease and have a great, stress-free trip if you keep these useful tips in mind.

GETTING TO KNOW BILBAO

Learn about the city's history, geography, local culture, and exciting events in order to appreciate Bilbao's beauty and culture to the fullest. To give you a better understanding of Bilbao, here is a brief overview:

- **History of Bilbao:** Bilbao has a lengthy, illustrious past. Initially a tiny fishing community, it progressively expanded during the 19th and 20th centuries to become a significant port and industrial hub. Bilbao is now regarded as a representation of urban renewal and groundbreaking architecture.

- Geographical characteristics and climate: Bilbao, located in northern Spain, is surrounded by beautiful natural scenery. The city is made more charming by the Nervión River's passage through it. a pleasant oceanic climate, with moderate temperatures, pleasant winters, and warm summers, prevails in the area. It's best to pack in accordance with the weather forecast for your trip.

- **Local Culture and Customs:** The Basque Country, where Bilbao is located, has its own unique culture and customs. Euskera, the language of the Basques, and their distinctive cultural history are things they are proud of. You can learn about Basque culture through music, dance, and sports. Locals are frequently seen having lively conversations, relishing delicious meals, and enthusiastically celebrating holidays.

- **Festivals & Events**: Bilbao is renowned for hosting exciting festivals and events all year long. The Aste Nagusia or Semana Grande, an August event with music, fireworks, and traditional Basque sports, is one of the highlights. The International Film Festival, the Santo Tomás Fair in December, and the Bilbao BBK Live music festival are a few further noteworthy occasions.

You'll understand Bilbao and its people better if you are familiar with the city's history, geography, customs, and cultural events. As you explore the city's attractions and engage with its inhabitants, this information will improve your overall experience and enable you to relate to the city on a deeper level.

History of Bilbao

The city of Bilbao has a long history dating back several centuries, growing from a tiny fishing community to a significant industrial and cultural hub. Here is a timeline of Bilbao's significant turning points in time:

- **Early Settlement**: People have lived in the region where Bilbao is located for a very long time. The first known settlement was a small fishing community called "Bilbao" that was founded on the banks of the Nervión River in the fourteenth century.

- Bilbao's strategic location close to the Bay of Biscay makes it a natural hub for maritime trade. Trade and Maritime Importance. The city started to thrive in the 15th and 16th centuries as a result of its trade with European markets, exporting products including wool, iron, and wine.

- **Industrial Revolution:** Bilbao's history saw a tremendous change throughout the 19th century. Rapid industrialization led to the city's development as a significant hub for mining, shipbuilding, and the production of iron and steel. The expansion of Bilbao's industrial sector was spurred by the development of the mining sector in the surrounding Biscay region.

- **Urban transition:** Bilbao had a dramatic transition with the growth of industrialization. To serve the expanding industries, factories, bridges, and infrastructure were built, reshaping the cityscape. During this time, many architectural icons were constructed, including the Mercado de la Ribera (Ribera Market).

- Bilbao had economic difficulties in the middle of the 20th century as a result of the demise of its traditional industry. But in the latter half of the 20th century, the city started a revitalization effort that was centred on urban renewal and the growth of the cultural and tourism industries.

- **The Guggenheim Effect:** The 1997 opening of the Guggenheim Museum Bilbao attracted attention from across the world and changed perceptions of the city. The museum, which was created by architect Frank Gehry, rose to fame as a symbol of modern architecture and served as a spark for the city's cultural resurgence.

- Bilbao is now praised for its effective urban redevelopment, innovative architecture, and a bustling cultural environment. Although the city's industrial past is still clearly visible, it has developed into a dynamic destination that blends tradition and contemporary and draws tourists from all over the world.

By visiting the Bilbao Historical Museum, which provides insights into the city's past, and touring the historic Casco Viejo (Old Town), with its winding alleyways and intact mediaeval buildings, one can expand their exploration of Bilbao's history.

Geography and Climate

The city of Bilbao is located in the Basque Country, an autonomous region of northern Spain. It is surrounded by beautiful scenery and is situated on the eastern shore of the Bay of Biscay. An summary of Bilbao's geography and climate is given below:

- Geographically, the Nervión River, which runs through the heart of the city, carved out a valley in which the city of Bilbao is located. The river finally empties into the Bay of Biscay, creating a natural harbour for Bilbao. Rolling hills and mountains can be found nearby, providing beautiful vistas and opportunities for outdoor sports.

- **Cityscape**: Bilbao is renowned for its distinctive fusion of contemporary construction and old sites. Frank Gehry's magnificent Guggenheim Museum serves as a testament to the city's development. The Euskalduna Palace, Iberdrola Tower, and Zubizuri Bridge are a few further prominent structures.

- **Climate**: Because of its proximity to the Bay of Biscay, Bilbao has a mild oceanic climate. The main features of Bilbao's climate are as follows:

- **Mild Winters**: From December to February, temperatures in Bilbao range from 8°C (46°F) to 13°C (55°F), which is considered to be mild. Rainfall is generally common, while snowfall is uncommon.

- Summers in Bilbao are warm and moderately humid (June to August). between 17°C (63°F) to 26°C (79°F), on average. It's important to remember that heat waves with temperatures in the 30s Celsius (80s to 90s F) might occur infrequently during the summer.

- **Spring and Autumn**: Bilbao enjoys a good climate from March to May and September to November. In these transitional times, temperatures range from 11°C (52°F) to 19°C (66°F).

- **Rainfall**: Bilbao experiences some rainfall throughout the year, with the fall and winter months seeing the most. It's a good idea to bring an umbrella or raincoat, especially if you go during the rainier seasons.

- **Outdoor Activities:** Outdoor lovers have a wide range of activities because of the various geography surrounding Bilbao. There are several popular hiking, climbing, and nature-exploring spots in the neighbouring mountains, including the Gorbea and Urkiola Natural Parks. Additionally, there are beaches and chances for water sports along the Bay of Biscay shoreline.

The topography and climate of Bilbao add to its allure and serve as a setting for a variety of outdoor and cultural experiences. Bilbao gives visitors an intriguing location all year long, whether you're exploring the city's architectural marvels or trekking into the surrounding natural splendour.

Local Culture and Customs

The Basque legacy has influenced Bilbao's unique culture and customs, which are found across the Basque Country of Spain.

The inhabitants, referred to as Bilbanos, are extremely proud of their customs, language, cuisine, and cordial hospitality. You may come across some of the following characteristics of local culture and customs when you visit Bilbao:

- **Basque Identity**: The Basques take great pleasure in their cultural heritage and sense of self. One of the earliest languages in Europe, Euskera, is the name of their own language. Even though Spanish is frequently used, particularly in more traditional places, you could hear locals speaking Euskera.

- **Gastronomy**: Bilbao is well known for its gastronomic scene, and the locals place a high value on food. In Bilbao, pintxos, the Basque equivalent of tapas, are well-liked.

There are many pintxos bars where you may enjoy a selection of small dishes matched with regional wines or cider. Additionally, Bilbao has a number of Michelin-starred eateries that serve as examples of the area's superior cuisine.

- **Festivals & Celebrations:** Throughout the year, Bilbao holds a number of festivals and celebrations that provide a window into Basque traditions and customs. The Semana Grande or Aste Nagusia, which takes place in August, is a week-long celebration with performances by musicians, dancers, firework displays, and athletes. The city comes alive at this season with exciting street entertainment and cultural events.

- **Sports in the Basque Country:** Basque sports, or "herri kirolak," are very important to the community. Popular sports like Basque pelota (a traditional ball game), wood-chopping contests, and stone-lifting contests are frequently displayed at festivals. These thrilling and well-known sporting events may be seen by you.

- **Sociability and Warmth:** Bilbao residents are renowned for their warmth and friendliness. It's customary to engage in conversation with residents, who are frequently eager to share knowledge of and suggestions for their city. Visitors are made to feel at home by the dynamic energy and active social scene of the city.

- Bilbao respects tradition and is proud of its long history and traditions. Basque folk music and dance performances are recognized as well as kept alive as traditional occasions. The inhabitants are glad to share their cultural history with guests and are proud of it.

- Bilbao is home to a large number of art galleries, museums, and craft studios that display Basque craftsmanship. You'll get the chance to discover and appreciate the artistic expression of the area, from traditional crafts like weaving, woodworking, and pottery to modern art displays.

- **Respect for the Environment**: The Basques have a strong love and respect for the natural world. The city of Bilbao is renowned for its efforts in environmental protection and sustainability. Eco-friendly procedures are used, and the area is dedicated to conserving its natural beauty.

You may engage with Bilbao's vibrant spirit and gain a deeper understanding of its people and traditions by embracing the local culture and customs. Your experience in this vibrant city will be enhanced if you respect the local way of life and are eager to get involved.

Festivals and Events

The Basque Country's rich culture, music, gastronomy, and traditions are celebrated year-round in the city of Bilbao, which is known for its love of festivities. Here are a few of Bilbao's major celebrations and occasions:

- The most anticipated festival in Bilbao is called Aste Nagusia (Semana Grande), which is held in August and translates to "The Great Week." There are sporting events, parades, fireworks, concerts, and other cultural and recreational activities throughout the week-long celebration. As residents and visitors congregate to enjoy the vibrant events, a joyous mood sweeps the city.

- **Bilbao BBK Live:** As one of Spain's most well-known music

events, Bilbao BBK Live draws eminent domestic and foreign performers. On the slopes of Mount Cobetas in July, it offers a singular location for music lovers to take in live performances of a variety of genres.
- The prestigious International Film Festival of Bilbao (ZINEBI) takes place every November. It provides a platform for up-and-coming filmmakers and celebrates the art of cinema by showcasing a variety of international short films and documentaries.
- Jazz fans travel to Bilbao every July to attend the Bilbao Jazz Festival. A number of concerts and performances by well-known jazz artists from throughout the world are part of the festival. The event displays the many rhythms and melodies of this genre in a number of locations throughout the city.

- **Santo Tomás Fair:** The Santo Tomás Fair is a customary Basque fair that takes place in Bilbao's Old Town every December. It includes booths offering traditional Basque crafts and goods as well as regional foods including cheese, veggies, and cider. Both locals and tourists are drawn to the colourful and joyful event.
- **Bilbao Maritime Festival:** Held in May, this festival honours the city's lengthy maritime heritage. Boat races, exhibitions, concerts, and sea-related events are all part of the festival. It's a great chance to discover Bilbao's relationship with the sea and take in some nautical-themed entertainment.

- **Bilbao Night Marathon**: The Bilbao Night Marathon, which takes place in October, is open to runners. Running through Bilbao's illuminated streets at night, taking in the city's sights and bustling ambiance, is a unique experience provided by the event.

- Basque Week is a collection of occasions and activities that celebrate Basque customs, music, dancing, and cuisine. It takes place in September. It's a wonderful chance to become fully immersed in the community's culture and get a sense of the Basque heritage.

These celebrations and events provide tourists an opportunity to celebrate, take in live performances, indulge in regional specialties, and participate in the bustling environment of Bilbao. They also give visitors a look into the vibrant and dynamic character of the city. When arranging your trip to Bilbao, be sure to verify the precise dates and schedules of these events.

PLANNING YOUR TRIP

It can be thrilling and satisfying to plan a trip to Bilbao. Careful planning will guarantee a pleasant trip, regardless of whether you are drawn to the city for its vibrant culture, architectural marvels, gastronomic delights, or scenic surroundings.

Here are some crucial suggestions to assist you in organising your vacation to Bilbao:

- Choose the Season and Weather that Suit Your Preferences to Determine the Best Time to Visit. The moderate climate of Bilbao makes it a year-round attraction, however the peak travel season is from June to August. While the winter months of December to February bring colder temperatures, the spring months of March to May and the fall months of September to November offer excellent weather with less tourists.

- Determine your intended stay in Bilbao depending on your interests and the activities you want to partake in. It is advised to spend at least 2-3 days exploring the city's top sights, but if you intend to travel farther afield or go to festivals, you might want to stay longer.

- **Research & Itinerary Planning**: To make a thorough itinerary, research the greatest sights, experiences, and attractions in Bilbao. The Guggenheim Museum Bilbao, Casco Viejo (Old Town), Ribera Market, Euskalduna Palace, and the Zubizuri Bridge are a few must-see locations. Don't forget to savour pintxos, sample the regional cuisine, and immerse yourself in the vibrant Basque culture.

- Choose the most appropriate method of transportation for your journey. An international airport, train stations, and public buses are all part of the well-connected transportation network in Bilbao. Think about whether you'll need to rent a car for day trips or use the city's public transportation system.

- **Accommodations**: Opt for lodging that matches your preferences and financial constraints. Luxury hotels, stylish inns, and inexpensive hostels are among the selections available in Bilbao. For convenient access to amenities and attractions, think about staying close to the city's heart.

- Although many locals in Bilbao understand English, knowing a few fundamental Spanish words can improve your relationships and demonstrate respect for the local way of life. Salutations, thank yous, and requests for directions can all be quite effective.

- Before travelling to Spain, make sure you have the proper travel documents and research the visa requirements for your country of residency. Check the validity of your passport and any other entrance restrictions.

- **Health and Safety:** As with any trip destination, safety and health must come first. Learn the local emergency numbers, carry any essential prescriptions, and stay informed of any unique travel or health alerts.

- **Payment and Currencies:** The Euro (EUR) is the currency used in Spain. Make sure you have access to cash or the appropriate currencies for small businesses. Despite the widespread acceptance of credit cards, it's a good idea to have some cash on hand for minor transactions or locations that might not accept cards.

- **Pack appropriately:** When preparing for your vacation to Bilbao, take into account the weather and the activities you'll be participating in. Bring proper clothing for the weather and comfortable shoes for walking about the city. A travel adapter, sunscreen, and a refillable water bottle are necessities that you shouldn't overlook.

You may plan a well-organised and pleasurable vacation to Bilbao by keeping these planning suggestions in mind. As you immerse yourself in the dynamic environment of this stunning Basque city, keep an open mind and provide space for unforeseen discoveries and unplanned excursions.

Best Time to Visit

Depending on your choices and the activities you intend to participate in, there is no one perfect time to visit Bilbao. To assist you in making a decision, the Bilbao seasons are broken down as follows:

- During the spring, when temperatures range from 11°C (52°F) to 19°C (66°F), Bilbao is at its most pleasant. Spring is from March through May. It's a wonderful time to explore outdoor attractions and take advantage of the city's parks and gardens as the city begins to bloom with beautiful flowers. In comparison to the summer, it is also less congested during this time.

- **Summer (June to August):** Bilbao's busiest travel period is the summer. With typical temperatures ranging from 17°C (63°F) to 26°C (79°F), the climate is warm. The city's beaches are wonderful right now, as are outdoor pursuits, festivals, and events like the Aste Nagusia. However, during this season, be prepared for more crowds and increased lodging costs.

- **Autumn (September to November):** Bilbao experiences excellent weather during the fall, with average highs of 11°C (52°F) and lows of 19°C (66°F). If you prefer a more laid-back environment, the city sees less visitors during the winter than during the summer. You can take part in cultural activities, see the city's museums, and take in the surrounding countryside's autumn splendour.

- **Winter (December to February):** The winter months in Bilbao are cooler, with highs averaging between 8°C (46°F) and 13°C (55°F). Even though it's the off-season for travel, this time of year has a certain beauty. You may take advantage of cheaper accommodation rates, experience the joyous holiday mood, and visit indoor attractions. Be aware that it may rain during the winter, so dress appropriately.

The best time to travel to Bilbao ultimately relies on your personal preferences for the weather, population density, and particular events or activities you intend to take part in. To get the most out of your trip to this bustling Basque city, think about your priorities and make travel arrangements appropriately.

Duration of Stay

Your hobbies, the activities you intend to undertake, and the amount of free time you have will all influence how long you should remain in Bilbao. When choosing the length of your stay, take into account the following factors:

- **City Exploration:** It is advised to spend at least 2-3 days getting to know Bilbao's top sights and experiencing its colourful culture. During this time, you can explore well-known attractions like the Guggenheim Museum Bilbao, stroll through the quaint alleyways of Casco Viejo (Old Town), and savour the city's world-famous culinary scene.

- **Day Trips:** Bilbao makes a great home base for exploring the area nearby. Consider including more days in your itinerary if you're interested in exploring areas outside of the city. You can take day trips to surrounding locations like the wine-producing region of La Rioja, the scenic Urdaibai Biosphere Reserve, or the coastal town of San Sebastian.

- **Festivals & Events:** Be sure to schedule enough time to explore and enjoy any festivals or events you intend to attend in Bilbao. It may take extra days to enjoy the activities and all the offerings at festivals like Aste Nagusia (Semana Grande) or Bilbao BBK Live.

- **Personal Preferences:** Take into account your desired level of immersion and your personal travel pace. If you prefer a more leisurely and laid-back visit, you might wish to extend your stay to thoroughly enjoy the place, find hidden gems, and partake in unplanned activities. A shorter visit, however, might nevertheless give you a taste of Bilbao's highlights if you have a packed schedule or little time.

The length of your stay in Bilbao will ultimately depend on your hobbies, free time, and travel choices. It's critical to create a balance between seeing the major sights of the city, providing time for leisure and cultural absorption, and leaving room for unanticipated discoveries.

Budgeting and Expenses

It's crucial to budget for your vacation and anticipate expenses while making travel plans to Bilbao to have a relaxing and pleasurable stay. When making a travel budget for your trip to Bilbao, keep the following things in mind:

- Bilbao provides a variety of lodging options to fit different budgets. There are high-end hotels, upscale inns, and inexpensive hostels. The pricing can change based on the location, the time of year, and the amenities offered. Find a place to stay that meets your interests and budget by researching and comparing several possibilities.

- A must-do when visiting Bilbao is to sample the local cuisine because the city is well-known for its gastronomic scene. Depending on where you choose to eat, the price of your meals may change. There are a variety of options available, from budget-friendly pintxos bars to fancy eateries. Pintxos, or Basque tapas, are a popular and affordable way to sample regional cuisine. Consider allocating funds to sample authentic Basque cuisine when dining out.

- Buses, trams, and a metro system are all part of Bilbao's well-connected transportation infrastructure. Your travel requirements and preferences will affect how much transportation will cost.

  Using a transit card or ticket can help you save money in Bilbao because public transportation is reasonably priced. Consider including additional transportation expenses in your budget if you intend to travel for day trips or to explore the area.

- Bilbao provides a wide range of attractions and activities, many of which charge an entrance fee. Your budget should account for the expense of visiting museums, art galleries, and famous sites like the Euskalduna Palace or the Guggenheim Museum Bilbao. Consider planning by looking into admittance costs and setting aside money for the sites and activities you want to partake in.

- Bilbao is renowned for its shopping avenues, boutiques, and regional markets. Make a shopping budget if you want to buy local goods, souvenirs, or traditional crafts. For fresh fruit, visit markets like Ribera Market, and for one-of-a-kind gifts, peruse the boutiques in Casco Viejo.

- **Festivals & Events:** If your visit to Bilbao falls during a festival or event, be aware that there may be extra fees for participating in or seeing specific performances or activities. To incorporate them into your budget, think about investigating the event schedules and any associated costs.

- Budget for extra costs like travel insurance, visa fees (if necessary), tips, and any additional activities or experiences you choose to include in your plan.

- Investigate Bilbao's average prices for lodging, dining, transportation, and activities to come up with a reasonable spending plan. Spend your money according to your priorities and personal preferences. It's usually a good idea to leave room in your budget for unforeseen costs or unplanned activities that may occur while you're travelling.

Finally, remember that a variety of budgets can be used to enjoy Bilbao. You can have a great and gratifying vacation in this energetic Basque city with careful planning and frugal spending.

Essential Travel Tips

To make the most of your vacation to Bilbao, consider the following vital travel advice:

- Plan your trip and do some study on the key sights, happenings, and traditions of the city before you go. Plan your trip after becoming familiar with the public transit system. Look into any unique exhibits or festivals that will be taking place while you are there.

- Although many locals in Bilbao understand English, learning a few basic Spanish words can improve your relationships and demonstrate respect for the local way of life. Simple salutations, "thank you," and "excuse me" can leave a good impression.

- **Respect Local practices**: The Basque culture has several traditions and practices that are significant to the neighbourhood. Be considerate of regional traditions, such as removing your hat before entering a church or observing quiet areas in public places.

- Although Bilbao is a relatively safe city, it's always vital to exercise common sense care. Keep an eye on your possessions, particularly when using public transportation or in crowded settings. Pay attention to your surroundings, especially at night. Additionally, it's a good idea to securely store a copy of your passport and other crucial papers.

- **Dress Properly**: Although Bilbao has a temperate climate, it's best to be prepared with layers of clothing in case the weather suddenly changes. For city exploration and walking, dress comfortably. Carrying a scarf or shawl to cover your shoulders if necessary is advised because visiting some holy places may demand modest clothes.

- **Enjoy the Local Cuisine:** Bilbao is known for its cuisine, therefore you must try some of it. Don't forget to try pintxos, the Basque equivalent of tapas, in neighbourhood bars. Be willing to sample regional specialties like txangurro (spider crab) and bacalao al pil-pil (codfish with garlic and olive oil).

- **Utilise Public Transportation**: Bilbao offers a reliable system of buses, trams, and a metro network for getting around town. To save money and enjoy convenience, think about purchasing a transportation card like the Barik card. A terrific method to get around the city and discover the surroundings is by using public transit.

- **Accept the Siesta Culture:** Be aware that some stores, particularly smaller ones, may close for a short period of time in the afternoon for the customary siesta break. Plan your activities accordingly and take use of the free time to unwind, eat in leisure, or wander through parks and gardens.

- Bilbao may get hot, especially in the summer, so make sure to stay hydrated and carry a water bottle. Carry a reusable water bottle to stay hydrated. It can be refilled at any of the city's countless fountains and taps.

While Bilbao has a lot to offer, think about exploring the surrounding area as well. Visit quaint coastal cities like San Sebastian, the Rioja wine region, or the scenic countryside on day outings. Because of its strategic location, Bilbao is a great starting point for touring the Basque Country.

When visiting Bilbao, keep in mind that you should be flexible, open-minded, and appreciative of the native way of life. Experience new things, immerse yourself in the lively atmosphere, and make enduring memories in this vibrant Basque city.

EXPLORING BILBAO'S NEIGHBOURHOODS

Each of Bilbao's dynamic, diversified neighbourhoods has a distinctive ambiance and attractions. The following are some areas worth visiting during your visit:

- **Old Town, or Casco Viejo**, is the centre of Bilbao and is distinguished by its winding alleyways, old structures, and quaint squares. Investigate the busy streets lined with stores, pubs, and eateries. Visit the Plaza Nueva, the Santiago Cathedral, and the Mercado de la Ribera, one of the biggest covered markets in Europe.

    Take advantage of the many bars that line the streets to enjoy pintxos or Basque tapas.

- **Ensanche (New Town)**, Bilbao's contemporary area, sits next to Casco Viejo and features broad roads and opulent structures. High-end stores, department stores, and hip eateries may be found here. The main street, Gran Va, is flanked by elegant shops and lovely buildings.

- Indautxu is a thriving area renowned for its busy atmosphere and economic activities. Visit the renowned cultural complex Azkuna Zentroa, which is built in a former wine warehouse. San Mamés Stadium, where Athletic Bilbao, the illustrious football team of the city, plays its home games, is also located in Indautxu.

- **Abando**: The Abando Train Station, Bilbao's primary transit hub, is located in this busy and vital area. Additionally, it is well known for the upmarket shopping area located at Gran Va de Don Diego López de Haro. Explore the local shops, cafes, and theatres as you stroll along the broad boulevards.

- **Deusto**: One of the most esteemed educational institutions in the city is located in Deusto, which is situated on the other side of the river from Casco Viejo. A combination of locals, students, and trendy eateries gives the area a young air. Views of the entire city can be had by visiting the stunning Deusto Bridge.

- **San Francisco**: San Francisco is a historic district with winding lanes, classic homes, and a bohemian vibe. It's a terrific location for exploring and finding undiscovered treasures like neighbourhood art galleries, independent stores, and quaint eateries. Views of the city are stunning from the Basilica of Begona, which is positioned on a hill.

- **Zorrozaurre**: Situated on an island in the Bilbao River, Zorrozaurre is a community that is rapidly developing. It is changing from an industrial region to a contemporary and artistic neighbourhood. Explore the galleries of modern art, stroll along the riverfront promenade, and take in the colourful street art that graces the area.

- Getxo is a neighbouring coastal town that is worth seeing even though it isn't legally part of

Bilbao. It has lovely beaches, a lovely marina, and a quaint ancient town. Explore the vibrant Algorta district while strolling along the well-known Puente Colgante (Hanging Bridge), a UNESCO World Heritage site.

A fresh perspective on Bilbao's cultural diversity and richness may be gained by exploring each of these areas, each of which has its unique personality and attractions. To get a true sense of the city, spend some time exploring and absorbing the distinct mood of each district.

Old Town (Casco Viejo)

Old Town, also referred to as Casco Viejo, is Bilbao's historic core and an area that every tourist should see. What to expect in this charming location is as follows:

- **Narrow Streets & Colourful Structures with Intricate Balconies**: Casco Viejo is distinguished by its winding, narrow streets that are dotted with vibrant structures. Mediaeval, Renaissance, and Baroque architectural styles all represent the region's long history. Admire the distinctive façade and architectural elements while strolling casually.

- Plaza Nueva is a bustling square that serves as the centre of activity in Casco Viejo. It has a neoclassical style and is surrounded by classy buildings with arcades. The plaza is a great place to unwind and people-watch because it is filled with several cafes, bars, and eateries. Here, a well-known flea market is held every Sunday.

- **Santiago Cathedral**: A notable feature in Casco Viejo is the Santiago Cathedral, often called the Cathedral of St. James. The interior of this Gothic-style cathedral, which was built in the fourteenth century, is exquisite, with spectacular stained glass windows and elaborate altarpieces. Take a moment to stroll around the tranquil cloister.

- One of the biggest covered markets in Europe is the Mercado de la Ribera, which is situated along the riverbank. You can take in the lively environment and shop for a wide selection of fresh fruits, vegetables, meats, cheeses, and regional delicacies here. It's a terrific spot to get acquainted with the regional culinary scene and sample authentic Basque products.

- **Bars that provide pintxos:** Casco Viejo is renowned for its thriving pintxos culture. The Basque Country's version of tapas is these tiny, tasty morsels. Numerous pintxos bars can be found lining the streets of the Old Town, where you can enjoy a range of scrumptious pintxos while sipping a cool glass of local wine or cider. It's a culinary experience you shouldn't pass up.

- The Teatro Arriaga is a magnificent neo-baroque theatre

that is situated in Casco Viejo. The theatre, which bears Juan Crisóstomo Arriaga's name, presents a range of cultural events, such as operas, ballets, and concerts. If you have the chance, check the schedule and attend a performance.

- **Bidebarrieta Library:** If you enjoy reading, you must stop by the Bidebarrieta Library. This public library, which is housed in a stunning neo-renaissance structure, has a large selection of books, journals, and multimedia resources. Even if you're not a big reader, the building itself is beautiful.

- **Events and Festivals:** Casco Viejo is a lively area that comes to life during events and festivals. If your visit coincides with the Aste

Nagusia (Semana Grande) in August, the streets of the Old Town will be packed with music, dance, and cultural acts. Throughout the year, the area also organises several events, so be on the lookout for any festivals taking place while you're there.

The distinctive atmosphere, historical sites, gastronomic treats, and cultural experiences of Casco Viejo make it one of Bilbao's must-see neighbourhoods. Spend some time exploring the area's lovely streets, indulging in pintxos, and learning about its fascinating history.

Ensanche

Ensanche, sometimes referred to as the New Town, is a bustling area of Bilbao that offers a contemporary and international vibe. The following are some of the neighbourhood's highlights:

- **Gran Vá:** The main avenue of Ensanche and a significant shopping district in Bilbao, Gran Vá. It's a wonderful location for shoppers, lined with attractive buildings and a variety of stores, from high-end boutiques to well-known brands. Explore the numerous stores, cafes, and restaurants along Gran Va while taking a stroll along it.

- Plaza Moya is the main square of Ensanche and is situated where Gran Va and the famous Alameda de Urquijo street meet. It has a lovely fountain and is encircled by famous structures like the Palacio Chávarri and the Iberdrola Tower. Due to its proximity to businesses, lodging options, and public transportation, the area acts as a gathering place and a focus of activity.

- Despite not being in Ensanche, the Guggenheim Museum in Bilbao is conveniently placed nearby and can be reached from the area. A must-see sight in Bilbao is this outstanding Frank Gehry architectural marvel. Discover the museum's collection of contemporary art, take in its distinctive façade, and take in the breathtaking views of the Nervión River.

- **Dona Casilda Iturrizar Park:** In the middle of Ensanche, this lovely park is a verdant haven. Dona Casilda Iturrizar Park, which bears the name of a well-known philanthropist from Bilbao, provides a tranquil haven away from the busy city streets. Enjoy a peaceful stroll along the walkways surrounded by trees, a seat on a bench, or a picnic here.

- **Albia Gardens:** The picturesque park of Albia Gardens may be found next to Plaza Moya. It has statues, well-kept gardens, and a charming central fountain. It's a wonderful spot to relax, especially on a bright day.

- **Gastronomy & Fine Dining**: Ensanche is home to a large number of upscale restaurants and eateries. If you want a fine dining experience, several choices highlight Basque cuisine and other world specialties. Savour the culinary creations and indulge in cutting-edge delicacies at one of the area's finest restaurants.

- Ensanche is home to several cultural and entertainment establishments. This area is home to the Bilbao Fine Arts Museum and its sizable art collection.

Additionally, there are theatres, movie theatres, and concert venues where you can see everything from plays to live music events.

- Ensanche frequently has a festive atmosphere, especially during festivals and events. The neighbourhood comes alive with holiday lights, decorations, and a joyful mood throughout the Christmas season. Holiday markets and live street entertainment bring the streets to life and create a spectacular atmosphere.

With its premium shopping, cultural attractions, and delectable cuisine, Ensanche offers a contemporary and vibrant experience in Bilbao. Spend some time getting to know this area, admiring its stunning architecture, and soaking in the lively atmosphere.

Abando

The downtown Bilbao district of Abando is well-known for its crowded streets, upscale stores, and cultural activities. Here is a sample of what the Abando neighbourhood has to offer:

- One of Bilbao's principal thoroughfares is Gran Via de Don Diego López de Haro, and the stretch that passes through Abando is especially well-known for its upmarket shopping. Along this busy route, explore a variety of boutiques, designer shops, and premium brands. It's a haven for people who love fashion and are looking for high-quality stuff.

- **Abando Train Station**: Also known as Bilbao-Abando or Estación del Norte, the Abando Train Station is a well-known transportation centre in the area. The station itself is a masterpiece of modernist and neo-Mudejar architecture. Before boarding a train to your next location, pause to take in its stunning facade.

- Azkuna Zentroa, formerly Alhóndiga Bilbao, is a distinctive cultural hub housed in a gorgeously renovated wine warehouse. This versatile theatre, created by famous architect Philippe Starck, holds concerts, film screenings, art exhibits, and more. In addition, it has a rooftop terrace, a pool, and a theatre, making it a lively and exciting area to explore.

- **Dona Casilda Iturrizar Park:** Located in Abando, this picturesque park is a lush haven in the middle of the city. This park features serene strolling trails, luscious vegetation, and a charming pond. It's the ideal location for unwinding, enjoying a picnic, or just taking in the natural beauty of the area.

- The Euskalduna Palace, one of the city's primary event locations, is a stunning architectural marvel that lies close to the waterfront. The skyscraper is a striking sight thanks to its modern style and glass façade. Check the schedule for events taking place in this renowned cultural centre, such as concerts, plays, conferences, and exhibitions.

- **Fine Dining and Gastronomy:** Abando is home to a huge selection of eateries, pubs, and cafes that provide a wide range of gastronomic options. You can discover something to suit every appetite, from authentic Basque food to global delicacies. Indulge in delicious cuisine and have a wonderful dining experience at one of the many restaurants in the area.

- **Ensanche area**: Abando easily flows into the nearby Ensanche area, where you can discover even more places to shop, go to shows, and see amazing buildings. Explore the bustling streets and broad boulevards of this contemporary neighbourhood on foot.

Don't pass up the opportunity to go to the famous Plaza Moya, the city's main square where numerous cultural events and celebrations are held.

- Abando is a fascinating area to discover in Bilbao since it combines elegance, cultural diversity, and entertainment opportunities. Take in the lively environment, enjoy culinary treats, and see the harmonious fusion of old and new features that characterise this busy region.

Indautxu

The lively neighbourhood of Indautxu is situated in the centre of Bilbao. Indautxu offers a wide variety of experiences and is well-known for its economic activity, lively environment, and notable landmarks. What you can find in Indautxu is as follows:

- Azkuna Zentroa is a cultural complex that acts as the focus of activities in Indautxu. It was once known as Alhóndiga Bilbao. This famous structure, created by Philippe Starck, has a distinctive architectural design. You'll discover live concerts, movie screenings, art exhibits, and a spectacular rooftop terrace within.

- Indautxu Square is a bustling community meeting spot in the area. This large square is encircled by cafes, restaurants, and shops, and it is embellished with lovely fountains. It's the perfect place to unwind, observe people, or sip coffee while taking in the energetic ambiance.

- San Mamés Stadium, the home field of Athletic Bilbao, one of Spain's most illustrious football clubs, is located in Indautxu. Catching a game here is a fantastic experience if you're a football enthusiast. If you can't make it to a game, you can still go to the stadium and check out the museum to learn more about the colourful past of the team.
- Gran Via de Don Diego López de Haro: The Gran Va neighbourhood, which extends along the Gran Via de Don Diego López de Haro boulevard, includes Indautxu. There are stores,

boutiques, cafes, and restaurants lining this upmarket street. It's a well-liked place for people who appreciate shopping and strolling leisurely in a lively environment.
- **Venues for Culture and Entertainment:** Indautxu is home to numerous places for culture and entertainment. A renowned theatre recognized for its varied schedule of plays, concerts, and other acts is the Campos Eliseos Theater. There are also plenty of options for cultural enlightenment in the area, including theatres, performance venues, and art galleries.
- **Shopping and Dining:** There are many different places to shop and eat in Indautxu. Discover specialty shops, boutiques, and fashion stores while strolling the neighbourhood's streets. You'll discover a mix of modern

restaurants serving a variety of delectable foods, traditional Basque cuisine, and cuisines from around the world when it comes to dining.
- **Accessibility**: Indautxu is easily accessible to other areas of the city thanks to its good transportation connections. A number of metro stations, bus routes, and tram stops in the vicinity make it convenient for you to explore Bilbao and the neighbouring places.

The bustling atmosphere of Indautxu, its proximity to San Mamés Stadium, its cultural amenities, and its shopping options make it one of Bilbao's most vibrant and active neighbourhoods.

Explore the cultural attractions, take in the local environment, become enamoured with football, and revel in the culinary treats that Indautxu has to offer.

Deusto

A lovely area called Deusto may be found in Bilbao on the Nervión River's right bank. It is renowned for its esteemed academic institutions, stunning architecture, and picturesque waterfront. Here are some of Deusto's highlights:

- **University of Deusto:** The University of Deusto is regarded as one of Spain's top academic institutions. It was established in 1886, is known for its academic brilliance, and provides a variety of programs. The campus is a work of art in terms of architecture, fusing old and new. Take a stroll around the campus to take in the stunning architecture and peaceful environment.

- **Puente de Deusto:** The Deusto Bridge, also known as the Puente de Deusto, is a well-known landmark in the area. Deusto and the city centre are connected by this beautiful suspension bridge that spans the Nervión River. To get a panoramic view of the river and the city skyline, cross the bridge. Particularly beautiful at sunset.

- The nautical Museum Ra de Bilbao is an interesting sight that highlights Bilbao's nautical history and is conveniently located close to the port.

Explore exhibitions on fishing, shipping, and shipbuilding, climb aboard an actual fishing vessel, and learn about the city's maritime history. The museum sheds light on the river's significance and how it shaped Bilbao's growth.

- Deusto Market is an active indoor market where you can discover a wide selection of fresh fruit, meats, fish, and regional goods. Discover the regional cuisines while interacting with merchants and soaking up the lively environment. It's a terrific spot to stock up on ingredients or try some mouthwatering treats.

- **Riverbank Walks:** Deusto has lovely riverbank paths that are great for a leisurely bike ride or stroll. Take in the beautiful river views, the waterfront's architecture, and the tranquil atmosphere. The pathways offer a peaceful haven from the busy metropolis.

- **Basque Culinary Center**: The Basque Culinary Center is a recognized organisation devoted to culinary instruction and research, and it is situated on the Deusto campus. It sponsors celebrations of Basque cuisine and provides training programs for aspiring chefs. Consider visiting the centre or going to one of its culinary events if you love food.

- Despite not being located in the centre of Deusto, the Euskalduna Conference Centre and Concert Hall is accessible by foot. Events ranging from conferences and conventions to concerts and performances are held in this beautiful location. To see whether any intriguing activities are taking place during your stay, check the schedule.

The combination of scholastic brilliance, cultural attractiveness, and scenic beauty is offered by Deusto. Discover the ancient university, take strolls along the river, explore the neighbourhood market, and take in the distinct charm of this area. It's a beautiful neighbourhood to explore amid the energetic city of Bilbao.

Getxo

In the Basque Country of Spain, Getxo is a picturesque beach town that lies close to Bilbao. What you need know about Getxo is as follows:

- **Beautiful Beaches**: Playa de Ereaga and Playa de Arrigunaga are just two of the breathtaking beaches in Getxo. These sandy beaches offer beautiful views of the Bay of Biscay and are the ideal location for swimming, water sports, and sunbathing.

- **Elegant Architecture**: Getxo, especially the Neguri area, is known for its beautiful architecture. Grand mansions and magnificent homes can be found here, serving as a reminder of the town's prosperous history. Explore the streets and take in the distinctive fusion of architectural styles.

- The famous Vizcaya Bridge (Puente de Vizcaya), a UNESCO World Heritage Site, is one of Getxo's top attractions. Getxo and the nearby town of Portugalete are connected by this unusual transporter bridge that dates to the late 19th century. Visitors can examine the bridge's intriguing history and engineering or take a gondola trip across the river.

- **Old Port**: The Old Port (Puerto Viejo) in Getxo is a lovely neighbourhood dotted with vibrant fishing boats, quaint seafood eateries, and waterfront walkways. It's a terrific spot for unwinding, dining al fresco, or taking a leisurely stroll along the marina.

- Getxo has lovely coastal walkways that let you take scenic walks along the cliffs and seashore. Coastal Walks. The attractive promenades are ideal for enjoying the cool sea wind and taking in the local scenery.

- The Biscay Transporter Museum, which is close to the Vizcaya Bridge, offers information about the construction and operation of the bridge. In addition to providing panoramic views from the tower and interactive exhibits about the bridge's construction and significance, it displays the original equipment used to build it.

- **Retail and dining:** Getxo has a bustling retail sector with a variety of boutiques, neighbourhood stores, and shopping malls. A broad variety of dining alternatives are available, including foreign cuisine, seafood specialties, and traditional Basque cuisine.

- **Cultural Events**: Throughout the year, Getxo offers a number of cultural events, such as music festivals, art exhibits, and customary Basque festivities. To discover whether any activities coincide with your stay, check the regional calendar.

- **Outdoor Activities:** Getxo has places where you may go biking, hiking, and doing water sports. You can rent bicycles to get around the town and its environs or go kayaking, paddleboarding, or surfing along the coast.

- The scenic Bridge of Bizkaia Maritime Walk connects Portugalete and Getxo over the river. It is a well-liked location for leisurely walks and photography since it provides breathtaking views of the Vizcaya Bridge and the surrounding area.

Getxo is a fascinating place to explore thanks to its combination of scenic natural features, interesting historical sites, and coastal charm. Getxo offers a distinctive and pleasurable experience around Bilbao, whether you're interested in beach activities, cultural events, or simply taking in the natural surroundings.o.

TOP ATTRACTIONS IN BILBAO

Northern Spain's bustling city of Bilbao is renowned for its extensive history, cutting-edge construction, and burgeoning cultural scene. The following are some of the top sights to see in Bilbao:

- **Guggenheim Museum Bilbao**: The Guggenheim Museum is a famous Frank Gehry architectural masterpiece. It presents transient exhibitions and is home to a notable collection of modern art. Explore the stunning artworks within while admiring the beautiful exterior's curving titanium panels.

- **Casco Viejo (Old Town):** Take a step back in time as you meander through Casco Viejo's winding streets. This attractive old district is full of vibrant buildings, mediaeval construction, and bustling squares. Explore historic attractions including the Santiago Cathedral and the Mercado de la Ribera, as well as boutiques and pintxos bars.

- **Plaza Nueva:** In the centre of Casco Viejo, there is a stunning square called Plaza Nueva. Neoclassical buildings surround it, and there are arcades, cafes, and eateries all around. The square is a well-liked gathering area and a terrific place to unwind and take in the ambiance.

- The Bilbao Fine Arts Museum is home to a sizable collection of Spanish and European artwork, including pieces by well-known creators including El Greco, Goya, and Picasso. Discover the wide variety of artwork from many centuries, including paintings, sculptures, and other forms of expression.

- The Arriaga Theatre is a venerable opera venue in Bilbao that bears the name of the esteemed composer Juan Crisóstomo de Arriaga. Admire the stunning architecture of this cultural centre and attend an opera, ballet, or theatrical performance.

- Visit the Mercado de la Ribera, one of Europe's biggest indoor markets, for more information. As you peruse the various stalls selling a variety of food items, try fresh fruit and local specialties and take in the lively environment.

- **San Mamés Stadium:** For fans of football, a trip there is a need. One of the oldest football clubs in Spain, Athletic Bilbao, calls it home. Take in the electrifying atmosphere of a game or a guided tour to discover the club's past and get a behind-the-scenes look.

- The Santiago Calatrava-designed Zubizuri Bridge, which crosses the Nervión River, is a stunning example of contemporary architecture. It is an impressive sight with its distinctively curved white construction and glass deck. Enjoy the views of the river and the skyline as you stroll casually across the bridge.

- Modern conference and performing arts facility Euskalduna Palace is situated close to the lake. It holds a variety of events, such as conferences, exhibitions, and concerts. To discover whether any intriguing events coincide with your visit, check the schedule.

- Doa Casilda Iturrizar Park offers a tranquil retreat from the hustle and bustle of the city. This urban haven includes peaceful walking trails, grassy areas, and a lovely pond. In the middle of the city, it's the ideal place to relax and take in the scenery.

These attractions only represent a small portion of Bilbao's offerings. Discover the city's distinctive fusion of old and new, delve into its thriving culture, and appreciate the gastronomic treats that make Bilbao such a spectacular location.

Guggenheim Museum

The Guggenheim Museum Bilbao is without a doubt one of Bilbao's most recognizable landmarks and a masterpiece of modern architecture. What you should know about this renowned museum is as follows:

- **Architectural Wonder:** The Guggenheim Museum Bilbao, which was created by renowned architect Frank Gehry, is in and of itself a piece of art. Large glass windows, curved titanium panels, and unusual organic shapes make up the building's stunning design. It has come to represent Bilbo's development into a major contemporary cultural centre.

- **Collection of Contemporary Art:** The museum is home to a substantial collection of contemporary works by Spanish and foreign artists. Famous painters including Jeff Koons, Andy Warhol, Mark Rothko, and Eduardo Chillida have pieces on display for you to enjoy. Various media, such as paintings, sculptures, installations, and multimedia artworks, are represented in the collection.

- **Temporary Exhibitions:** The Guggenheim Museum Bilbao presents temporary exhibitions that feature the creations of contemporary artists from all over the world in addition to its permanent collection. There is always something fresh and intriguing to learn about thanks to the varied viewpoints and theme studies offered by these shows.

- **Architectural Details:** Pay attention to the museum's distinctive architectural details as you explore the space inside. A centre area with curved walkways and a lofty glass roof that lets in natural light is the atrium, also referred to as The Flower. Because the museum's galleries are connected, visitors can move easily between the various display areas.

- **Outdoor Sculptures**: There are a number of impressive outdoor sculptures all around the museum that enhance the artistic environment. The most well-known is "Puppy," a sizable topiary sculpture by Jeff Koons that is shaped like a West Highland White Terrier and is covered in colourful flowers.

Richard Serra's "The Matter of Time" and Anish Kapoor's "Tall Tree & The Eye" are two further noteworthy outdoor works of art.

- **Restaurants and Museum Shop**: The Guggenheim Museum Bilbao has a museum shop where you may discover uncommon gifts, publications, and design items related to art. A number of cafes and restaurants are also located inside the museum, giving visitors a chance to unwind and have a meal or drink while admiring the surroundings.

- Lectures, workshops, and performances are just a few of the cultural events that the museum organises throughout the year. These gatherings offer extra chances to interact with art and learn more about modern artistic techniques.

An unique experience, the Guggenheim Museum Bilbao mixes stunning architecture with intriguing modern art. The museum is certain to make an impression and pique your aesthetic curiosity, whether you're an art connoisseur or simply admire cutting-edge design.

Santiago Cathedral

The majestic religious landmark Santiago Cathedral, commonly referred to as the Cathedral of Santiago de Bilbao, is situated in the centre of Bilbao's famed Casco Viejo (Old Town). What you need to know about this magnificent church is as follows:

- **Historical Importance:** The 14th-century Santiago Cathedral is of significant historical and cultural value to Bilbao. The city's patron saint, St. James the Apostle, is honoured by its dedication.

- The cathedral's architecture is mostly in the Gothic style, with Renaissance and Baroque features as well. Its stunning stone facade, which is covered in complex sculptures and artistic accents, defines its outside. A prominent aspect of the church is the tower, often known as the Arriaga Tower.

- **Highlights of the Interior:** Enter Santiago Cathedral to view the stunning interior. The nave is lofty and roomy, with magnificent columns and high ceilings. Be careful to take in the cathedral's beautiful stained glass windows, which let in vibrant light. The interior's splendour is further enhanced by the high altar, chapels, and elaborate religious artwork.

- Santiago Cathedral is a significant resting place on the Way of St. James, a well-known pilgrimage route that leads to Santiago de Compostela. The cathedral attracts pilgrims from all over the world and is a great representation of religious fervour and devotion.

- **Relics and artefacts:** The cathedral is home to a number of religiously significant relics and artefacts. The Santo Cristo de la Salud, a wooden sculpture of Christ that is thought to have healing abilities, is one prominent relic. Spend some time exploring the chapels and side altars where you can discover more gems and sacred art.

- **Religious Services:** Religious services are often held at the busy site of worship known as Santiago Cathedral. If you go during a service, you can see how pious everyone is and hear the gorgeous organ playing fill the church.

- **Plaza Santiago:** Plaza Santiago is a lovely square next to the cathedral where locals and tourists congregate. Enjoy a peaceful moment on the square while being surrounded by the stunning church and the historic Casco Viejo buildings.

You can understand the historical, architectural, and spiritual significance of this magnificent holy building by going to Santiago Cathedral. Explore the interior at your own pace, take in the revenant ambiance, and marvel at the skill that went into building this magnificent structure.

Arriaga Theater

In the centre of Bilbao, there is a historical and cultural treasure called Teatro Arriaga Antzokia. What you need to know about this famous theatre is as follows:

- **History and architecture:** The Arriaga Theater, which bears the name of famed Basque musician Juan Crisóstomo de Arriaga, was constructed in 1890. Neoclassical, Renaissance, and Baroque influences may be seen in the theatre's architecture, which combines several different architectural styles. It is a well-known landmark in the city due to its exquisite exterior and opulent interior.

- Opera, ballet, drama, concerts, and other artistic events are all performed regularly at the theatre, which is a thriving centre for culture. The Arriaga Theater presents a varied program that appeals to a variety of creative inclinations, ranging from concerts of classical music to contemporary dance productions.

- **Opera Season:** Opera productions have a long history at the Arriaga Theater. You may catch outstanding productions of well-known operas during the opera season, performed by talented artists, accompanied by a full orchestra and stunning settings. You can get a chance to see the majesty of opera up close and the impact of live performances.

- Ballet and dance performances are also presented at the theatre by national and international companies. On stage, take in the magnificent choreography, delicate gestures, and captivating storyline. The Arriaga Theater provides a stage for a variety of dance expressions, from classical ballet to modern dance styles.

- **Theater Productions**: At the Arriaga Theater, take in the beauty of live theatre. Various theatrical works, including plays, musicals, and avant-garde performances, are presented at the theatre. Whether it's a period piece or a modern drama, you can count on superb performances, gripping stories, and immersive set designs.

- **Guided Tours:** The Arriaga Theater offers tours that give information about its past, present, and hidden facets. Learn about the theatre's role in Bilbao's cultural environment as you tour the auditorium, foyers, and backstage areas.

- **Café & Restaurant:** Before or after a play, you can unwind, eat, or have a drink in the theatre's café or restaurant. It's a terrific place to soak up the creative energy and interact with other theatre fans regarding the arts.

The Arriaga Theater serves as both a performance space and a representation of Bilbao's rich cultural history. It provides a chance to see works by renowned artists and experience the allure of live performances. A trip to the Arriaga drama is sure to be a special occasion whether you enjoy opera, ballet, drama, or simply the arts in general.

Bilbao Fine Art Museum

The Museo de Bellas Artes de Bilbao, also known as the Bilbao Fine Arts Museum, is a renowned art gallery that is situated in Bilbao, Spain. What you should know about this cultural treasure is as follows:

- **Highlights of the Collection:** The Bilbao Fine Arts Museum is home to a sizable collection of European and Spanish artwork from various centuries. It includes artwork dating from the Middle Ages to the present, with a focus on Basque and Spanish painters. Paintings, sculptures, prints, and decorative arts are all part of the collection.

- **Spanish Masters:** Famous Spanish artists El Greco, Francisco de Goya, Diego Velázquez, and

Pablo Picasso are represented in the museum's collection. You can gaze upon their works of art and learn about how Spanish art has changed over time.

- A chance to study the distinctive artistic manifestations of the Basque region is offered by the museum's significant collection of Basque art. Learn about the works of well-known Basque artists like Eduardo Chillida, Jorge Oteiza, and Ignacio Zuloaga.

- **International Artists:** The museum exhibits work by international artists in addition to Spanish and Basque art. Paintings from artists including Peter Paul Rubens, Claude Monet, Vincent van Gogh, and Francis Bacon are among those you can see. You are able to recognize various artistic influences and styles because of this diversity.

- **Temporary Exhibitions**: The Bilbao Fine Arts Museum frequently presents temporary exhibitions that examine certain subjects, trends, or artists while providing new insights on the visual arts. These shows offer a chance to learn more about various artistic contexts and discover new works.

- **Architectural Setting**: The museum is housed in a stunning structure that combines features of both classical and modern architecture. The expansive galleries where the artwork is displayed are reached through the grand entrance and neoclassical façade. The architecture of the museum offers a befitting setting for the works of art it houses.

- Workshops, tours, lectures, and other educational programs are all provided by the museum with the goal of fostering visitors' appreciation for and knowledge of art. These activities offer beneficial experiences for both individuals and groups and are catered to various age groups.

- The Bilbao Fine Arts Museum has a museum shop where you can buy art books, exhibition catalogues, one-of-a-kind presents, and copies of works of art. There is also a café where you may unwind, sip some coffee, and think back on your trip to the museum.

You can discover a wide variety of artistic expressions and dig into the realm of art by visiting the Bilbao Fine Arts Museum. This museum offers an enthralling voyage through the worlds of Spanish, Basque, and European art, whether you're an art aficionado, a history lover, or simply interested in cultural heritage.

Zubizuri Bridge

The stunning Campo Volantin Bridge, commonly referred to as the Zubizuri Bridge, crosses the Nervion River in Bilbao, Spain. What you should know about this miracle of architecture is as follows:

- **Architecture and Architecture:** The Zubizuri Bridge, created by renowned architect Santiago Calatrava, is a remarkable illustration of contemporary bridge architecture. It has a distinctive curving, suspended frame that gives it a classy, futuristic look. The bridge's construction in steel, glass, and white concrete adds to its modern appearance.

- **Friendly to Pedestrians**: The Nervion River can be crossed safely and amicably by pedestrians only on the Zubizuri Bridge. Its design prioritises giving walkers a seamless and relaxing experience so they may enjoy the scenery while they cross the bridge.

- The bridge's pedestrian deck is built of white concrete tiles, giving it a striking and modern appearance. The bridge's overall aesthetic appeal is improved by the smooth surface, which is also nice to walk on.

- **Suspension and Arch**: On one side of the river, a suspension arch is used to support the Zubizuri Bridge. The bridge gains solidity and structural integrity thanks to this architectural detail, which also offers a visually arresting aspect that blends in with the surroundings.

- Transparent glass balustrades flank the sides of the bridge, providing unhindered views of the river and the surrounding area. This architectural decision not only increases safety but also gives the bridge a feeling of openness and lightness.

- **Integrity with the Environment**: The Zubizuri Bridge is built to aesthetically complement its surroundings. Its contemporary design harmonises with the nearby Guggenheim Museum's modern architecture to produce a seamless visual experience along the riverbank.

- **Famous sight**: The Zubizuri Bridge is a well-known sight in Bilbao that draws both residents and tourists. It is a well-liked destination for photography, strolls, and taking in the picturesque views of the river and the city due to its distinctive design and strategic location.

A stop at the Zubizuri Bridge is essential whether you're taking a stroll along the riverbed or touring adjacent sights like the Guggenheim Museum. You may enjoy the inventive design and architectural splendour that make Bilbao a city recognized for its modern aesthetic through this visually spectacular and pedestrian-friendly experience.

Alhóndiga Cultural Center

The Spanish city of Bilbao is home to the bustling Alhóndiga Cultural Center, sometimes referred to as Azkuna Zentroa. What you need to know about this special location is as follows:

- **Background information:** The Alhóndiga Cultural Center is housed in an old structure that was constructed in 1909. It was first built as a wine storage but has now changed to become a vibrant cultural centre.

- **Architectural Redesign:** The renowned French architect Philippe Starck repaired and remodelled the structure. His plan preserved some of the existing architectural features while transforming the area into a modern, multipurpose cultural centre.

- Various artistic areas are available for use in various cultural activities in the Alhóndiga Cultural Center. These include galleries, a theatre, a movie theatre, and a library. It is a flexible location for cultural activities because the many areas cater to visual arts, performing arts, film screenings, and literary endeavours.

- **Contemporary Art Exhibitions:** The centre presents recurring exhibitions of contemporary art that feature the creations of regional, international, and local artists. The exhibitions feature works in a variety of artistic mediums, such as photography, sculpture, painting, and multimedia installations.

- **Cinematic Experiences**: The Alhóndiga Cultural Center has a cutting-edge theatre that shows a wide range of movies. Film aficionados can enjoy a wide variety of cinematic experiences at the movies, from mainstream blockbusters to independent films and documentaries.

- **Theatre Shows:** The theatre in the centre hosts a range of theatrical productions, such as plays, dance performances, and music concerts. It gives both homegrown and outside performers a stage on which to display their skills and captivate audiences with provocative performances.

- **Library and Media Center**: The Alhóndiga Cultural Center is home to a cutting-edge library with a sizable selection of printed materials, periodicals, and online sources. It also has a media centre where guests can access digital and audiovisual products.

- **Recreational Areas:** The centre provides areas for relaxation and interaction. These include a fitness centre, a swimming pool, and a rooftop patio with expansive city views. These places encourage guests to take part in physical activities and relax occasionally.

- **Gastronomic Options:** The Alhóndiga Cultural Center offers a wide range of dining establishments, including eateries, coffee shops, and bars. These places provide a wide variety of cuisines, allowing customers to delight in both domestic and foreign cuisine.

- **Cultural Programming:** To promote creativity and cultural awareness, the centre offers seminars, lectures, and other educational programs as part of its cultural programming. The centre is an inclusive and interesting place for the community thanks to these programs, which cater to people of all ages and interests.

The Alhóndiga Cultural Center united art, culture, leisure, and education in a vibrant and stimulating setting. The centre provides visitors from all walks of life with a colourful and educational experience, regardless of their interests in visual arts, performing arts, movies, literature, or simply looking for a place to unwind and socialise.

OUTDOOR ADVENTURES AND NATURE

The region around Bilbao is home to many outdoor activities and chances to get back in touch with nature. Here are some things to do and places to visit in nature:

- **Hiking and mountainous landscapes:** The stunning mountains and natural parks that surround Bilbao offer fantastic chances for hiking and trekking. To find picturesque pathways, luxuriant forests, and spectacular vistas, visit locations like Gorbea Natural Park, Urkiola Natural Park, or Armaón Natural Park.

- **Coastal Exploration**: Bilbao is situated along the breathtaking

Bay of Biscay coastline. Explore the scenic beaches, cliffs, and coastal trails on foot or by renting a bike. Plentzia Beach, Sopelana Beach, and the rough shoreline close to the Gaztelugatxe islet are all well-liked locations.

- **Sports on the water**: The Bay of Biscay provides excellent conditions for a variety of water sports. At beaches like Mundaka and Bakio, which are renowned for their exceptional surf breaks, surfers can catch waves. In order to soak in the seaside landscape, you may also try paddleboarding, kayaking, or even go on a boat tour.

- Avid bird watchers can find paradise in the area surrounding Bilbao. Diverse bird species can be found in the Urdaibai Biosphere

Reserve, which is close to the city. Explore the wetlands and marshes and look out for herons, spoonbills, and other waterfowl.

- **Riding Routes:** The city of Bilbao and its surrounds provide a variety of riding routes for cyclists of all skill levels. Whether road riding or mountain biking is more your style, you may explore picturesque landscapes and quaint settlements. Popular options include the Zalla Greenway and the Bilbao-Bilbao bicycle path.

- Rock climbing is a popular activity for thrill-seekers in the neighbouring mountains. There are numerous climbing routes available in places like Peas de Oro, Monte Albertia, and El Pagasarri that are appropriate for climbers of all levels.

Always take the necessary safety precautions, and if you're unfamiliar with the activity, think about hiring a guide.

- **Exploring caves:** There are several interesting caverns in the area that are worth seeing. Visit locations like Santimamie Cave, which has prehistoric cave drawings, or Pozalagua Cave, which is renowned for its beautiful stalactite formations.

- **Natural Reserves:** Outside of Bilbao, there are various protected areas and natural reserves that are worth visiting. Some examples of the breathtaking natural landscapes just waiting to be found include the Urkiola Natural Park, Ordesa and Monte Perdido

National Park, and the Picos de Europa National Park.

You may immerse yourself in the area's natural beauty and partake in exhilarating activities thanks to these outdoor activities and natural attractions close to Bilbao. There are many options to get back in touch with nature in and around Bilbao, whether you're looking for an exhilarating adventure or a peaceful getaway.

Mount Artxanda

Near the Spanish city of Bilbao, Mount Artxanda is a beautiful hill. What you need to know about this well-known attraction is as follows:

- **Spectacular Views:** From Mount Artxanda, you may enjoy a beautiful panorama of Bilbao and its surrounds. The city's skyline, the Nervion River's twisting course, and the lovely surroundings that lie beyond may all be seen from the summit.

- **Funicular access:** Taking the Artxanda Funicular is one of the simplest methods to get to the peak. You may take a convenient and delightful journey up the hill on this old cable railway while taking in the beautiful scenery along the route.

- **Recreational Area:** The recreational area of Mount Artxanda draws both locals and tourists. A sizable park with well-kept green areas, strolling trails, and picnic places may be found on the summit. It's the ideal place to unwind, enjoy a picnic, or engage in outdoor activities.

- **Hiking and Nature paths:** Mount Artxanda has a variety of hiking and nature paths for those looking for an active trip. You can get some exercise while exploring the hill's forested regions and taking in the peace of nature. There are several levels of difficulty on the well-marked routes.

- Tennis courts and a golf course are among the sporting amenities that may be found on Mount Artxanda's hillside. Visitors can participate in leisure pursuits, play competitive games with their friends, or just enjoy watching sports.

- **Restaurants and cafes:** At Mount Artxanda's peak, there are a number of eateries and cafes where you can relax with a meal or a beverage while admiring the breathtaking views. It's a wonderful chance to enjoy the regional food and unwind in a tranquil environment.

- **Cultural Attractions:** The Basilica of Begona, a stunning Gothic-style church with religious and cultural significance for the residents, is another cultural attraction on Mount Artxanda. During your time on the hill, it is worth visiting because of its impressive architecture and extensive history.

A trip to Mount Artxanda offers a welcome diversion from the hustle and bustle of the city, whether you decide to take a leisurely stroll, set off on a trekking expedition, or just soak in the beautiful scenery. It is a well-liked vacation spot for both residents and visitors because it provides the ideal balance of scenic beauty, recreational activities, and cultural attractions.

Dona Casilda Park

In the centre of Bilbao, Spain, is Dona Casilda Park, also known as Parque de Dona Casilda Iturrizar, a picturesque urban park. What you should know about this lovely green area is as follows:

- Doa Casilda Park provides a tranquil haven away from the busy metropolis. Visitors can rest, relax, and get away from the bustle of the city in this beautiful oasis' rich vegetation, peaceful ambiance, and well-kept gardens.

- **Gorgeous Gardens:** The park has expertly maintained gardens with a variety of plant species, vibrant flowers, and big trees that cast shade and foster a relaxing atmosphere. Explore the park's vegetation as you stroll along the trails.

- **Location**: Doa Casilda Park is conveniently located close to the city's core and is a well-liked hangout for both locals and visitors. When visiting Bilbao, its handy location makes it the perfect spot for a rest, a picnic, or a leisurely stroll.

- **Water Attractions:** The park has a number of attractive water attractions. Ducks and swans can be seen gliding across a tiny lake and there are fountains, ponds, and even a few fountains. The tranquillity and natural beauty of the park are enhanced by these attractions.

- **Sculptures and Monuments**: The park is filled with sculptures and monuments that enhance the aesthetic and cultural significance of the area. These installations act as focus points and offer intriguing places to explore and learn more about.

- **Children's Play Area**: Dona Casilda Park features a designated children's play area that is furnished with play structures, swings, and other amusements. It's a great place for families where kids can play and get some energy out.

- The park occasionally holds events and activities, including outdoor concerts, exhibits, and cultural festivals. These activities give the park more life and provide visitors the chance to participate in social gatherings and enjoy live entertainment.

- **Recreational Possibilities**: Dona Casilda Park provides chances for outdoor pursuits. Along the designated trails, you may jog, ride a bike, do yoga on the grass, or just find a quiet area to read a book and enjoy the sunshine.
- The park is conveniently accessible to several other well-known attractions in Bilbao. It is simple to combine a trip to Dona Casilda Park with a trip to the Guggenheim Museum or a stroll along the close-by Gran Va, a busy street noted for its stores, cafés, and energetic environment.

Doa Casilda Park provides a scenic location and a welcome break from Bilbao's metropolitan environment, whether you're seeking for a quiet retreat, a place to enjoy nature, or a site to spend quality time with family and friends.

Urdaibai Biosphere Reserve

Near Bilbao, Spain, in the Basque Country sits the breathtaking natural area known as the Urdaibai Biosphere Reserve. It is famous for its remarkable biodiversity and distinctive ecological value, and UNESCO has designated it as a biosphere reserve. What you need to know about this amazing place is as follows:

- **Awe-inspiring Natural Beauty**: The Urdaibai Biosphere Reserve is home to a wide variety of flora and fauna, including marshes, estuaries, woods, and meadows. These habitats work together to produce an ecosystem that is both aesthetically pleasing and ecologically diverse.

- **Important Bird Area**: With such a wide diversity of avian species living there, the reserve is a birdwatcher's delight. It has been recognized as an Important Bird Area (IBA) and offers several bird species, especially migratory birds, a critical habitat for nesting, resting, and feeding.

- **Protected Wildlife:** Several protected species, including the endangered Iberian desman and the European mink, can be found in the Urdaibai Biosphere Reserve. The reserve is essential to the preservation of these species and their habitats, which benefits biodiversity as a whole.

- **Coastal Wonders:** The reserve's coastal regions are home to stunning views and striking geological wonders. With its marshes and tidal flats, the Urdaibai estuary provides a rich environment and a feeding area for numerous bird species.

- **Hiking and nature paths:** The reserve has a system of clearly marked pathways that let visitors enjoy its natural beauties. There are paths ideal for all levels of fitness and interests, whether you like leisurely strolls or strenuous excursions. These routes give you the chance to fully experience the varied landscapes and get up close to the local flora and creatures.

- Sustainable development and environmental education are priorities for the Urdaibai Biosphere Reserve. It provides educational programs and initiatives to increase tourists' and local populations' understanding of the value of biodiversity conservation and to encourage sustainable practices.

- **Cultural heritage**: The reserve is a culturally significant site in addition to being a natural gem. It includes ancient structures, archeological monuments, and typical Basque fishing communities, giving visitors a glimpse into the area's rich cultural legacy.

- **Recreational Activities:** The Urdaibai Biosphere Reserve offers a variety of recreational opportunities for visitors. Birdwatching, kayaking or canoeing along the estuary, biking along the approved trails, or just finding a picturesque site for a picnic while admiring the breathtaking surroundings are all enjoyable activities.

- **Visitor Centers**: The reserve offers informational centres where you may learn about the natural and cultural history of the region. To help you better comprehend and appreciate the distinctive features of the reserve, these centres offer educational exhibits, tours, and other materials.

- **Tourism that is Sustainable:** The Urdaibai Biosphere Reserve encourages visitors to preserve nature, stick to approved pathways, and patronise nearby establishments that adhere to sustainable ideals.

A trip to the Urdaibai Biosphere Reserve is a wonderful chance to get in touch with nature, learn about various ecosystems, and see how crucial biodiversity conservation is. The reserve's breathtaking landscapes and natural treasures are likely to captivate your senses whether you're an enthusiastic nature lover, a bird enthusiast, or simply looking for a quiet vacation.

Bilbao's Beaches

Despite being a large city, Bilbao is fortunate to have several lovely beaches nearby. Here are a few of the well-known beaches close to Bilbao:

- One of the most well-liked beaches close to Bilbao is Playa de Ereaga, which is situated in the neighbouring town of Getxo. A lengthy stretch of golden sand, crystal-clear water, and breathtaking views of the Bay of Biscay are all present there. The beach is well-suited for swimming and sunbathing because it has facilities like lifeguard coverage, showers, and beach bars.

- **Playa de Arrigunaga:** Playa de Arrigunaga is a beautiful beach in Getxo that is close to Playa de Ereaga. It is renowned for its picturesque cliffs and rock formations, which provide beachgoers with a dramatic background. Families will enjoy the beach's amenities, which include parking, seaside eateries, and restrooms.

- Playa de Plentzia is a large sandy beach that is surrounded by magnificent mountains and is found in the charming coastal town of Plentzia. It offers a tranquil environment that is perfect for sunbathing, beach activities, and strolls along the shore. The beach is close by and provides facilities like beach bars, showers, and restrooms.

- **Playa de Sopelana**: Slightly outside of Bilbao, Playa de Sopelana is well known for its top-notch surf conditions. Surfers from all over the world travel to this expansive sandy beach to catch the powerful waves. You can still take in the stunning views and a cooling dip in the ocean even if you don't surf.

- **Playa de Azkorri:** Also known as Barinatxe Beach, Playa de Azkorri is a well-liked surfing location close to Playa de Sopelana. It has a sizable sandy beach and spectacular cliffs on either side. Compared to the metropolitan beaches closer to Bilbao, the beach is more serene and feels more rugged.

These beaches close to Bilbao offer a great chance to unwind, take in the sunshine, and participate in water sports. These coastal treasures provide a welcome respite from the city and an opportunity to take in the natural splendour of the Bay of Biscay, whether you prefer swimming, sunbathing, or catching some waves.

GASTRONOMY AND NIGHTLIFE

Getxo and its neighbouring areas have a wonderful culinary scene and fascinating nightlife alternatives. Gastronomy and nightlife are dynamic components of Basque culture. Here's what to anticipate:

Gastronomy:

- **Pintxos**: Getxo is well-known for its delicious pintxos, as does the rest of the Basque Country. These little, bite-sized culinary treats, which highlight the region's culinary ingenuity, are frequently served on a slice of bread and topped with a variety of ingredients.

Discover the pintxos bars in Getxo's town centre and savour the Basque cuisine's tastes.

- **Seafood:** Getxo is well-known for its fresh seafood because it is a beach town. You can choose from a variety of seafood meals, including grilled fish and delectable shellfish. Don't pass up the chance to sample classic Basque meals like chipirones en su tinta (squid in ink sauce) and marmitako (tuna stew).

- **Traditional Basque Cuisine:** Some restaurants are serving traditional Basque food in Getxo. Discover the flavours of substantial stews, grilled meats, and regional specialties like ganguro (stuffed crab) and bacalao al pil-pil (codfish in garlic and chilli sauce).

- Traditional cider houses, or "sagardotegi," can be found in the nearby region of Astigarraga. At these eateries, you can sample the regional cider straight from the barrel while also indulging in a hearty meal of grilled steak, cod omelette, and other cider house favourites.

Nightlife:

- **Bars and Pubs**: The bar scene in Getxo is vibrant, especially in the town centre. There are many taverns and pubs to choose from, with anything from craft beers and unique cocktails to regional wines and ciders. Enjoy the welcoming environment, mingle with the people, and take in the exciting nightlife.

- Getxo is home to several music venues where live performances of jazz, rock, and traditional Basque music are held. If there are any performances or events that coincide with your visit, check the local listings. These places provide you with the chance to experience the rich musical history of the area.

- **Bars on the coastline**: During the summer, Getxo's coastline comes alive with bars and clubs. As you stare out at the beach and the water, sip on a cool beverage, dance to upbeat music, and soak up the celebratory ambiance.

- **Late-Night Socialising:** Basque culture places a high priority on getting together with friends and family, frequently well into the wee hours of the morning. At bars, cafes, and outdoor terraces, you'll have lots of chances to strike up talks with residents and other tourists.

Getxo and the neighbouring villages provide an exciting dining and nightlife scene that let you immerse yourself in the colourful Basque Country culture.

Getxo offers plenty to offer everyone's tastes and preferences, whether you're exploring the pintxos bars, enjoying fresh seafood, or immersing yourself in the vibrant atmosphere of the pubs and music venues.

Traditional Basque Cuisine

Rich flavours, top-notch ingredients, and culinary skills that have been handed down through the years are hallmarks of traditional Basque cuisine. The region's rich natural resources, including the sea, mountains, and lush farmland, are reflected in the cuisine of the Basque country.

The following are some essential ingredients and meals that define traditional Basque cuisine:

- **Pintxos**: A staple of Basque cuisine, pintxos are little, bite-sized dishes. Usually placed on a slice of bread and held together with a toothpick, these tasty little morsels are compact and portable. Pintxos are available in a wide range of flavours, from straightforward pairings like ham and cheese to more complex dishes made with fish, meats, and vegetables.

- **Fresh fish:** The Basque Country's proximity to the shore provides a plentiful supply of fresh fish. Hake, sea bass, anchovies, and cod are just a few of the fish dishes found in Basque cuisine. Popular seafood meals include grilled fish, marmitako (a tuna and potato stew), and bacalao al pil-pil (codfish in a garlic and pepper sauce).

- **Txakoli Wine:** Txakoli is a typical Basque wine that is well-known for its crisp and energising qualities. It goes well with shellfish and pintxos, and on a warm day, its crisp acidity makes it a great choice. The Basque region is where txakoli is largely manufactured, and each subregion has its unique style.

- Cheeses from the Basque Country are renowned for being prepared from the milk of sheep, cows, or goats. Two well-known Basque kinds of cheese with a rich, distinct flavour are idiazabal and local. You can eat these cheeses by themselves or as a part of a cheese board with quince paste and walnuts.

- **Taloak**: Traditional Basque pancakes made from corn that can be stuffed with a variety of toppings are known as taloak. They frequently contain chorizo, cheese, or veggies and provide a filling snack or quick supper.

- **Chuletón**: Chuletón is the name for a big, thick-cut ribeye steak that is usually grilled or cooked over an open flame. Chuletón is a classic illustration of the Basque Country's love of grilled meats. The region is known for its premium cattle. A juicy and tasty steak is produced when it is simply salted and grilled to perfection.

- **Marmitako**: Made with fresh tuna, potatoes, onions, peppers, and tomatoes, marmitako is a classic Basque fisherman's stew. It is a rich and comforting dish that showcases the region's long-standing culinary traditions and close ties to the sea.

- **Gâteau Basque**: Often enjoyed with a cup of coffee or as a sweet treat after a meal, Gâteau Basque is a typical Basque dessert made of buttery, crumbly pastry filled with either custard or a traditional black cherry preserve called "confiture de cerise noire."

These are but a few of the numerous mouth watering dishes that make up traditional Basque cuisine. Additionally, Basque chefs and eateries are renowned for their dedication to utilising fresh, in-season ingredients and cutting-edge cooking methods while respecting the area's gastronomic tradition.

A pleasant excursion into the rich culinary tapestry of the Basque Country is discovering traditional Basque cuisine.

Pintxos Culture

The culture of pintxos is fundamental to Basque social life and culinary legacy. Small, bite-sized snacks or appetisers known as pintxos are frequently placed on a slice of bread and held in place with a toothpick. They are frequently savoured with a beverage, such as a crisp lager or a glass of wine.

Pintxos are more than simply a specific kind of cuisine; they stand for a distinctive social and culinary tradition that is ingrained in Basque culture. Following are some salient features of pintxos culture:

- Pintxos are available in a variety of flavours, ingredients, and presentations. When it comes to pintxos, there is no dearth of diversity, ranging from straightforward pairings like cured ham and cheese to more intricate arrangements including fish, meats, and vegetables. Cooks and chefs take pride in their ingenuity and are always experimenting with new culinary combinations.

- **Pintxos Bars**: Scattered across Basque villages and cities are pintxos bars, where pintxos are generally consumed. These establishments focus on serving a large variety of pintxos that are presented on the bar counter. The bar staff will count the toothpicks on your plate to determine your final bill while you take your time selecting the pintxos that appeal to you.

- Pintxos bars are dynamic social hubs where locals and visitors assemble. They are more than just places to dine. People frequently converse while having pintxos with friends and coworkers while standing at the bar. Because of their welcoming atmosphere, pintxos pubs are a great place to get to know locals, learn about their culture, and become immersed in Basque life.

- **Bar Hopping**: The practice of moving from one pintxos bar to another while sampling various pintxos and cocktails is known as "going on a pintxo crawl" or "doing the trinitro" in the pintxos culture. It's an enjoyable pastime that lets you sample the cuisines of other restaurants.

- Pintxos are frequently paired with a glass of the region's wine or cider. Excellent wines from the Basque Country, such as Txakoli, Rioja Alavesa, and Getariako

Txakolina, go well with pintxos. Additionally, "sagardotegi" or cider houses offer a singular experience where you can drink traditional Basque cider while consuming pintxos and a substantial lunch.

- **Seasonality & Fresh Ingredients**: Fresh, seasonal ingredients are highly valued in the pintxos culture. The finest local ingredients are used by chefs and cooks to make pintxos that highlight the regional flavours. Pintxos honour the diversity of Basque cuisine, featuring anything from just caught seafood to seasonal vegetables and cured meats.

- **Tradition and Innovation**: The culture of pintxos is a synthesis of both. While traditional pintxos with time-tested pairings are still enjoyed, chefs are also pushing the envelope of originality by bringing fresh flavours and preparation methods to the pintxos industry. Pintxos culture remains vibrant and dynamic thanks to this harmony between tradition and innovation.

Every trip to the Basque Country must include experiencing pintxos culture. It enables you to experience the local cuisine, interact with locals, and become fully immersed in the lively social scene. So take a toothpick, visit some pintxos bars, and set off on a gourmet journey that will reveal the essence of Basque cooking.

Best Restaurants and Bars

There are several choices available to fit every taste and inclination when it comes to the greatest bars and restaurants in Bilbao. Bilbao has much to offer for everyone, whether you're looking for modern dining experiences, traditional Basque food, or busy bars. Some of the best eateries and bars in the city are listed below:

Restaurants:

- **Azurmendi**:Three-Michelin-star eatery outside of Bilbao, Azurmendi provides an extraordinary dining experience with its cutting-edge food and environmentally conscious ethos.

  The restaurant's spectacular architecture and lovely views add to the overall experience, which is enhanced by the dishes that Chef Eneko Atxa prepares using ingredients that are found locally.

- **Mina** is a Michelin-starred restaurant serving up contemporary and inventive Basque fare in the centre of Bilbao. A dish created by chef Alvaro Garrido demonstrates his culinary prowess by fusing conventional flavours with cutting-edge preparation methods.

- **Nerua**: Chef Josean Alija runs the Michelin-starred restaurant Nerua, which is housed in the Guggenheim Museum. The restaurant emphasises using fresh and nearby sources to produce aesthetically pleasing and delectable dishes.

- El Perro Chico serves up traditional Basque food with a contemporary spin in Bilbao's Old Town (Casco Viejo). El Perro Chico is a well-liked alternative for both locals and visitors due to its friendly atmosphere and menu, which includes delicacies like slow-cooked meats, fish, and inventive pintxos.
- The well-known restaurant Boroa Jatetxea is situated in a picturesque rural environment close to the town of Amorebieta-Etxano. It creates outstanding dishes by fusing traditional Basque ingredients with cutting-edge cooking methods, and the warm, inviting ambiance enhances the eating experience.

Bars:

- Café Irua is a classic bar with a classy, traditional environment that is located in the heart of the city. Since 1903, it has served as a gathering place for residents and guests, serving a variety of drinks such as cocktails, wines, and spirits.
- **La Ribera:** La Ribera is a well-known location for pintxos and drinks that is close to the Ribera Market. It is a favourite among both locals and visitors due to its lively environment, a wide variety of pintxos, and a well-stocked bar.
- **El Globo** is a renowned Old Town pub with a lively ambiance and welcoming staff. It has a wide selection of pintxos and beverages, and its outside patio is a perfect area to take in the bustling Casco Viejo streets.

- **La Via del** Ensanche is a typical pub with a welcoming environment that is well-known for its delicious pintxos. It is located in the Ensanche area. It provides a wide range of alternatives, from traditional pintxos to cutting-edge inventions.
- **Bar Txakoli** is a well-known location to savour the customary Basque wine, txakoli, and is situated in the Indautxu area. Enjoy a range of pintxos and other Basque cuisines with a cool glass of txakoli.

The top eateries and bars in Bilbao include places like these. The city has a thriving culinary scene that provides a variety of opportunities to explore and savour the flavours of Basque cuisine, sip on a cool beverage, and take in the lively ambiance that distinguishes Bilbao's eating and bar culture.

Nightclubs and Entertainment

With a wide range of nightclubs and entertainment alternatives to suit all preferences, Bilbao has a vibrant nighttime scene. Bilbao offers something for everyone, whether you prefer live music, partying the night away, or seeing distinctive cultural shows.

Here are some of the city's most well-liked bars and entertainment spots:

- **Fever Club:** A well-known nightclub with a vibrant ambiance and a wide variety of music genres, Fever Club is situated in the centre of Bilbao. For a wonderful night of dancing and entertainment, it offers various themed nights with DJ performances, live bands, and special events.

- Cotton Club is a well-known nightclub that draws a diverse clientele. It is located in the Indautxu district. Electronic, pop and Latin rhythms are among the musical genres available, and both national and international DJs are present.

- **Move it! Bilbao**: This energetic nightclub in the Old Town (Casco Viejo) is renowned for its jovial atmosphere and diverse musical tastes. Move it! often throws themed parties and events and plays a variety of music, including pop, rock, indie, and electronic.

- Kafe Antzokia is a well-known music venue that features live performances by regional and international performers. It is situated in the Abando district. Kafe Antzokia offers a varied

selection of musical experiences in a distinctive and intimate atmosphere, from jazz and folk shows to rock and pop concerts.
- **Bilborock**: Bilborock is a cultural and youth centre that hosts a variety of events, such as live music performances, DJ sets, and art exhibits. It has a large following of music lovers since it features up-and-coming local talent and presents a diversity of musical styles.
- **Azkena**: An established music venue that hosts live performances by regional and international musicians, Azkena is located in the Ensanche district. It is known for showcasing independent and alternative music, drawing a wide range of music fans.
- **Teatro Arriaga:** Teatro Arriaga is a location that you just must see

if you're interested in experiencing the performing arts. It is a stunning theatre in the heart of the city that presents a variety of acts, such as opera, ballet, dramas, and classical music concerts.

- **Bilbao Exhibition Centre (BEC):** The Bilbao Exhibition Centre is a well-known location for larger-scale events, concerts, and exhibitions. All through the year, it hosts big events like conventions, trade shows, and concerts from around the world.

It's important to keep in mind that Bilbao's nightlife culture is dynamic and subject to change. You may keep up with the most recent venues, events, and performances taking place in the city while you're there by checking local event listings, getting recommendations from locals, or reviewing online resources.

SHOPPING IN BILBAO

The shopping environment in Bilbao is broad and includes everything from chic boutique shops to old-fashioned markets. There are many options available to fulfil your shopping needs, whether you're seeking for high-end clothing, regional handcrafted goods, or one-of-a-kind souvenirs.

Here are some of Bilbao's well-known shopping destinations and stores:

- **Gran Va:** One of Bilbao's main shopping avenues, Gran Va is lined with a variety of boutiques, department stores, and specialty businesses. Popular fashion labels, accessories, cosmetics, and other items can be found here. It's a busy area with a mix of domestic and foreign retailers.

- **Zubiarte**: A contemporary shopping area with a range of stores, including fashion boutiques, electronics shops, home furnishing stores, and a sizable supermarket, is situated close to the city centre.

It provides a relaxing shopping environment with a variety of services, restaurants, and a movie theatre.

- **Casco Viejo:** Bilbao's picturesque Old Town, also known as Casco Viejo, is where you can find a ton of speciality stores and boutiques. Discover unique stores selling handcrafted crafts, regional goods, jewellery, and traditional Basque items as you wander through its winding lanes. It's a terrific spot to shop for genuine trinkets and get a taste of the local culture.

- Located in the heart of the city, Moyua Square is flanked by posh stores and boutiques. Reputable multinational brands, high-end fashion retailers, and designer labels can all be found here. It is a centre for upscale shopping and provides a chic retail environment.

- **Mercado de la Ribera:** The largest covered market in Europe and a veritable haven for foodies, the Ribera Market is located in the city of Barcelona.

There are specialty food stores that sell regional specialties such as cheeses, spices, and meats in addition to the main emphasis on fresh fruit, meats, and seafood. It's a fantastic location to browse local ingredients and take in the lively ambiance of a traditional market.

- **Corte Inglés:** In Spain, a well-known retail chain is the El Corte Inglés department store. The Bilbao location, which is in the heart of the city, provides a huge range of goods, including apparel, accessories, cosmetics, home goods, technology, and fine foods. You may fulfil all of your buying needs here.

- The area of Bilbao La Vieja has grown to be a centre for independent boutiques, art galleries, and antique shops. Explore its streets to locate one-of-a-kind clothing treasures, vintage things, vinyl records, and locally produced art.

- **Deusto**: There are a number of small stores and boutiques in the Deusto area that sell a variety of clothes, accessories, and lifestyle goods. Shopping here is more peaceful than in the busy city centre.

Always check the store hours before you go shopping and make your plans appropriately. Whether you're looking for the newest fashions, vintage trinkets, or regional delicacies, Bilbao's varied retail culture has something for everyone.

Shopping Districts

There are a number of distinctive shopping areas in Bilbao that provide distinctive experiences and accommodate various shopping preferences. Each neighbourhood has its own unique charm and specialisations, giving customers a range of options. The following are some popular retail areas in Bilbao:

- One of Bilbao's biggest shopping avenues is Gran Vá, which is situated in the centre of the city. Department stores, fashion businesses, and local and worldwide brands are all represented.

    For those seeking a variety of retail alternatives in a convenient location, this bustling area is ideal.

- **Casco Viejo**: Bilbao's Old Town, also known as Casco Viejo, is a bustling neighbourhood with attractive stores and winding streets. Traditional clothing boutiques, artisanal craft stores, and speciality stores may be found here.

  They sell Basque goods, such as gourmet treats and handcrafted trinkets. Casco Viejo is the perfect location for experiencing local culture while browsing specialty stores.

- **Ensanche**: The Ensanche neighbourhood, commonly referred to as the "new town," is a contemporary and affluent region with a mixture of upmarket clothing boutiques, high-end brands, and designer shops. This neighbourhood's broad streets and magnificent buildings contribute to the area's upscale shopping vibe.

- **Moyua Square:** Located in the Ensanche neighbourhood, Moyua Square is a well-liked retail zone with upmarket jewellery shops, notable fashion boutiques, and well-known worldwide brands. This square draws fashion fans looking for high-end brands and serves as a centre for luxury shopping.

- Indautxu is a thriving area with a range of stores that cater to various requirements. It has a variety of local enterprises, specialty shops, small boutiques, and fashion retailers. This area is well-known for its variety of shopping opportunities, making it a fantastic place to browse various shops and find hidden gems.

- **Zubiarte**: Zubiarte is a cutting-edge shopping centre close to the city's core. It has a wide variety of stores, including clothing boutiques, electronics shops, supermarkets, and movie theatres. With several attractions under one roof, this mall offers a convenient and enjoyable shopping experience.

- **Abando**: Abando is a bustling neighbourhood where you may go shopping, conduct business, and have fun. A variety of commercial establishments, including department stores, clothing boutiques, book stores, and speciality shops, may be found here. Abando is a convenient shopping destination because it is well-connected and accessible.

These shopping areas provide distinct atmospheres and accommodate a range of shopping interests. The several shopping areas in Bilbao offer a wide variety of possibilities to discover and enjoy, whether you're seeking for distinctive locally produced goods, upscale brands, or cutting-edge shopping malls.

Unique Souvenirs and Crafts

There are many locally produced goods that highlight the culture, artistry, and craftsmanship of the city when it comes to unique gifts and crafts in Bilbao. You can find the following examples of distinctive crafts and mementos in Bilbao:

- Look for traditional Basque items that showcase the area's diverse cultural heritage. These could include handcrafted leather goods, ceramics, woodwork, jewellery, and fabrics that have been wove by hand.

  These products are available at regional craft markets or at artisanal stores in the Casco Viejo (Old Town).

- **Txakoli Wine**: Made in the Basque Country, Txakoli is a crisp, delicious white wine. Wine lovers would be wise to take home a few bottles of this regional wine. It can be purchased directly from regional vineyards in the surrounding area or in specialised wine shops.

- **Gourmet Food Items:** Bilbao is well-known for its cuisine, and there are many gourmet food items that make wonderful gifts. A few things to look for include Basque cheeses, artisanal chocolates, olive oils, tinned seafood (such as anchovies or bonito), and "pastel vasco" (Basque cake), which is a typical dessert.

- **Basque Berets**: The Basque beret is a recognizable cap that has

been linked to the area for many years. A real Basque beret is a fashionable and genuine souvenir made of high-quality materials. In Bilbao, you may locate them in boutiques or specialty hat stores.
- **Bilbao Art Prints**: Bilbao has a thriving art scene, and you can get posters and prints of notable buildings like the Zubizuri Bridge and the Guggenheim Museum. To take a piece of Bilbao's creative appeal home, look for local art galleries or gift stores that sell prints created by local artists.
- **Instruments from the Basque region:** Music plays a significant role in Basque culture, and authentic Basque instruments make for interesting gifts. Look for percussive instruments like the txalaparta, Basque accordions like the trikitixa, and wind instruments like the .

These can be acquired in Bilbao from traditional instrument makers or speciality music stores.
- Books written in the Basque language, Euskara, are a good place to start if you're interested in learning more about the language and culture of the Basques. These can offer fascinating insights about the culture, language, and history of the area.

Investigate the neighbourhood markets, artisan stores, and specialised shops in Bilbao if you're looking for one-of-a-kind gifts and crafts.

Particularly renowned are the numerous shops in Casco Viejo that sell authentic Basque items. In addition, keep an eye out for any neighbourhood fairs or events where artists and craftspeople exhibit their creations, since these may be fantastic places to find one-of-a-kind items.

DAY TRIPS FROM BILBAO

A great place to start your exploration of the Basque Country's surroundings is Bilbao. From Bilbao, you may take day trips to a number of lovely locations, where you can see the area's varied topography, rich cultural history, and stunning coastline.

Here are a few well-liked day excursion ideas:

- San Juan de Gaztelugatxe is a beautiful island with a charming hermitage perched on top, and it's only about an hour's drive from Bilbao. A stone bridge links the island to the mainland, and it provides stunning views of the untamed coastline. Fans of the television show "Game of Thrones" and those who enjoy the outdoors frequent this location.

- **San Sebastián:** A coastal treasure located just one hour by rail from Bilbao, San Sebastián is famed for its gorgeous beaches, quaint Old Town, and vibrant culinary scene. Visit the famous Comb of the Wind sculptures, wander along La Concha Beach, and savour pintxos (Basque tapas) at the many bars and eateries.

- Vitoria-Gasteiz is a historic city with a well-preserved mediaeval centre and serves as the capital of the Basque Country. Visit the majestic Santa Maria Cathedral in Gothic architecture, stroll through the winding alleyways, and take in the serene ambiance of the city's parks and green areas.

- Not to be mistaken with San Juan de Gaztelugatxe, Gaztelugatxe is another gorgeous beach town around 40 minutes from Bilbao. It has a hermitage on top of a small islet that is connected to the mainland by a meandering stone walkway. The views of the Bay of Biscay and the neighbouring rocks are spectacular.

- The Urdaibai Biosphere Reserve is a UNESCO Biosphere Reserve with a distinctive natural setting that is around 30 minutes from Bilbao. Discover the charming fishing community of Mundaka, go surfing at the world-famous Mundaka Wave, and take in the varied wildlife of the marshes and estuary.

- **Rioja Wine area:** The Rioja wine area, which is about an hour and a half's drive from Bilbao, is worth visiting if you're a fan of wine. Visit wineries for tastings, tour the vineyards, and discover how the famed Rioja wines are made.

- **Getxo**: A seaside city with lovely beaches, opulent promenades, and the recognizable Vizcaya Bridge, a UNESCO World Heritage site, Getxo is only a short metro trip from Bilbao. Take a leisurely stroll along the sea, explore the picturesque Old Port, and ride the extraordinary swinging bridge.

These are only a few of the numerous day trip alternatives that are offered from Bilbao. The Basque Country provides a range of experiences close to the dynamic metropolis of Bilbao, whether you're interested in nature, culture, or gastronomy.

San Sebastian

A gorgeous coastal city in northern Spain's Basque Country, San Sebastian is also known as Donostia in Basque. It is well known for its magnificent beaches, top-notch culinary scene, and quaint Old Town.

Following are some highlights and tips for visiting San Sebastian:

- **La Concha Beach**: A crescent-shaped cove with smooth golden sand and crystal-clear blue waves, La Concha Beach is regarded as one of the most stunning urban beaches in all of Europe. Enjoy the breathtaking views of the sea and the surrounding hills while taking a leisurely stroll down the promenade or unwinding on the beach.

- **Old Town (Parte Vieja):** San Sebastián's Old Town is a charming maze of winding alleyways brimming with lively pintxo bars, regional stores, and historic structures.

Take in the city's renowned pintxos, the Basque equivalent of tapas, while strolling the streets and sipping on some Txakoli wine from the region.

- Hike up Monte Urgull for sweeping views of the city and its shoreline. The Castillo de la Mota, a castle from the 12th century that today functions as a museum, can be found at the peak. View the spectacular views of San Sebastian and the Bay of Biscay while exploring the castle grounds.

- **Monte Igueldo:** Monte Igueldo is another hill that provides stunning views of the city. Take the funicular up to the summit, where you may look out from the tower and take in the view. Visit the old-fashioned amusement park at the summit, which still exudes an air of antiquity and has attractions for both kids and adults.

- **Kursaal Congress Center:** The Kursaal Congress Center is a prime example of San Sebastián's modern architecture. The famed San Sebastián International Film Festival is one of many cultural events held in this remarkable structure created by renowned architect Rafael Moneo.

- Head to Zurriola Beach if you want to experience a more vivacious and upbeat beach environment. It is a surfers' favourite location since it has great waves and a thriving beach culture. Beach volleyball and beachside eateries are also available.

- **Mount Ulia:** For those who enjoy the outdoors, a hike along Mount Ulia is a wonderful way to see San Sebastián's scenic surroundings. The magnificent routes along this coastal mountain range provide sweeping views of the city, the ocean, and the surrounding countryside. It's the perfect getaway for outdoor pursuits and tranquil strolls.
- The San Telmo Museum, which is housed in a former Dominican convent, presents the rich history and culture of the Basque Country. It offers insights into the history of the area through its assortment of

archaeological objects, traditional Basque art, and modern exhibitions.
- **Food & gastronomy**: San Sebastián is known for its Michelin-starred restaurants, authentic pintxo bars, and fresh seafood. It is a gourmet heaven. Don't pass up the chance to enjoy the city's culinary treats, which range from Michelin-starred meals to pintxo hopping in the Old Town.
- San Sebastián is a must-see location in the Basque Country because of its natural beauty, vibrant culture, and culinary offers. San Sebastián will fascinate and enchant you with its appeal and beauty whether you're looking for relaxing on the beach, exploring old streets, or indulging in world-class food.

Vitoria-Gasteiz

The picturesque and ancient city of Vitoria-Gasteiz, located in northern Spain's Basque Country, is renowned for its preserved mediaeval core, lovely gardens, and thriving cultural scene. Following are some highlights and tips for visiting Vitoria-Gasteiz:

- The ancient old town of Vitoria-Gasteiz, known as Casco ancient, is the city's beating heart. Explore its winding streets, which are dotted with protected ancient structures, picturesque squares, and quaint stores. Visit the city's central plaza, Plaza de la Virgen Blanca, and take in the famed white monument there.

- **Santa Maria Cathedral:** The Santa Maria Cathedral, a 13th-century masterpiece in the

Gothic style, is situated in the old town. Visit the spectacular interior, including the cloister, on a guided tour, and climb the cathedral tower for sweeping views of the city.

- **Plaza de Espana:** Both locals and tourists congregate in this bustling square. Sip coffee while taking in the ambience at one of the outdoor cafes, or just unwind on a bench and people-watch. The stunningly designed Basque Parliament building is also located in the area.

- The Artium Museum is a noteworthy museum of modern art located in Vitoria-Gasteiz. Explore this gallery's varied collection of modern and contemporary art, which includes creations by both Basque and foreign artists. Additionally, the museum sponsors cultural activities and transient exhibitions.

- **Green Spaces**: Vitoria-Gasteiz was named the "Green Capital of Europe" in 2012 due to its abundance of green spaces. Visit the Parque de la Florida, a lovely park with a pond, fountains, and brilliant flowerbeds.

The renowned monument of "El Espíritu del Jardin " (The Spirit of the Garden), a fictional character created by Ken Follett, is also located in the Parque de la Florida.

- **Murals**: Vitoria-Gasteiz has an outstanding array of murals painted all throughout the city. Discover these colourful and thought-provoking murals that grace the exterior of buildings and showcase the creativity of local and international artists by going on a self-guided tour or signing up for a guided tour.

- The Basque Museum of Contemporary Art (Artium) is a museum of modern and contemporary art that exhibits a variety of media, including painting, sculpture, photography, and installations. The museum is a must-visit for art fans because it often offers cultural events and exhibitions.

- **Gastronomy**: Vitoria-Gasteiz has a wide range of modern restaurants, pintxo bars, and traditional Basque restaurants. Try regional specialties like pintxos (Basque tapas), customary stews like marmitako, and renowned

Rioja wines from the area's wine region.

- Vitoria-Gasteiz is a beautiful city to explore because of its rich history, cultural legacy, and green landscapes. Take your time exploring the town's lovely streets, indulging in the cuisine, and getting acquainted with the laid-back Basque way of life.

Rioja Wine Region

Northern Spain is home to the Rioja wine region, which is mostly in the autonomous community of La Rioja but also stretches into sections of the Basque Country and Navarre.

One of the most well-known and respected wine areas in the world, it is famed for its superb red wines, breathtaking vineyards, and long-standing winemaking customs. An overview of the Rioja wine region is provided below:

- Wine tastings and excursions are available at many of the wineries in the Rioja wine area, which welcomes guests. Learn about the winemaking process, see both historic and contemporary wineries, and savour a selection of Rioja wines, including the renowned Tempranillo. Make reservations in advance at the majority of vineyards before visiting.

- **Haro** A fantastic place to start your exploration of the region is the town of Haro, which is known as the "wine capital" of Rioja. Visit the famous Haro vineyards, including López de Heredia and Muga, which provide tastings and guided tours. The Batalla del Vino, an annual wine competition conducted in Haro on June 29th, is another reason for its fame.

- **Logrono**: The capital of La Rioja, Logroo, is a great place to start your exploration of the area. Explore the city's picturesque streets and vibrant tapas bars to sample the mouthwatering pintxos and local wines. The Calle Laurel and Calle San Juan, known for their culinary offerings, should not be missed.

- **Wine Museums**: By visiting the different wine museums in the area, you may better comprehend the history and culture of winemaking in Rioja. One of the most extensive museums dedicated to the history, art, and science of winemaking is the Vivanco Museum of Wine Culture in Briones.

- **Vineyard Scenery**: Investigate the beautiful Rioja vineyard scenery while you can. The area is renowned for its picturesque landscape, which includes undulating hills, vast vineyards, and attractive villages. Think of going to the picturesque towns of

Laguardia, Labastida, and Briones, which are encircled by vineyards.

- **Wine Routes:** There are a number of wine routes available in the Rioja wine region, offering well-planned itineraries for visiting various locations and wineries. There are three sub-regions of Rioja: Rioja Alta, Rioja Alavesa, and Rioja Oriental. Each has unique features and wineries to explore.

- **Wine Festivals**: You're in for a treat if you visit during one of these events. Throughout the year, the area holds a number of wine-related events, such as the San Mateo Wine Harvest Festival in Logrono, where you can take in wine tastings, parades, concerts, and customary festivities.

- **Wine and Gastronomy Pairing:** Rioja is renowned for both its wines and its delectable cuisine. Enjoy the local fare, which includes lamb chops, roasted peppers, and seasoned anchovies. Many wineries now provide wine-pairing events where you may eat regional cuisine while sipping their wines.

Wine lovers and those seeking a distinctive cultural and culinary experience should explore the Rioja wine area. The Rioja wine area offers an extraordinary voyage into the world of Spanish wine, whether you decide to tour historic wineries, immerse yourself in breathtaking vineyard scenery, or savour the regional delicacies.

Santander

Northern Spain's Cantabria region has the thriving coastal city of Santander. Santander, which is well-known for its stunning beaches, interesting landmarks, and lively atmosphere, provides visitors with a wide variety of sights and activities to enjoy.

This is a guide to getting about Santander:

- One of the most well-known and visited beaches in the city is **Playa del Sardinero**, where you may unwind at the beginning of your trip. Enjoy the sunshine, go swimming, or just stroll lazily along the promenade and take in the breathtaking coastline views.

- The **Palacio de la Magdalena** is a famous palace in Santander that is perched on a beautiful peninsula. Discover the palace's majestic architecture, stroll through its lovely gardens, and take in the expansive views of the Bay of Santander. Throughout the year, the palace also hosts cultural gatherings and exhibitions.

- **Centro Botin**: At the magnificent Centro Born, a cultural hub created by famous architect Renzo Piano, immerse yourself in modern art. Visit one of its stunning art exhibits, take in a play or concert, or just relax on its rooftop terrace and take in the expansive views.

- **Santander Cathedral:** In the centre of the city, you can find the magnificent Santander Cathedral, a masterpiece of Gothic architecture. Explore the cathedral's lovely interior and marvel at the spectacular altarpiece as you admire the exterior meticulous detailing.

- The Paseo de Pereda is a picturesque waterfront promenade that is adorned with lovely structures, gardens, and sculptures. Take a leisurely stroll along it. Take in the relaxing ambiance, a coffee or a snack at a café, and the views of the water.

- Discover the charming park, Jardines de Piquio, which is perched on a cliff overlooking the sea. Relax on the benches, take a leisurely stroll around the well-kept gardens, and take in the spectacular views of the seaside.

- The Cantabrian Sea's biodiversity and maritime history are both covered in the museum known as the Marine Museum of the Cantabrian Sea. Learn about the region's nautical past via exciting exhibits that feature marine life, historical artefacts, and interactive displays.

- **Mercado del Este:** The Mercado del Este is a bustling market where you can discover fresh vegetables, regional specialties, and traditional crafts. Here, you can experience the colourful local culture. Experience the vibrant atmosphere of this historic market while sampling regional specialties.

- Explore Monte Buciero, a nature reserve renowned for its panoramic splendour and hiking paths, by taking a quick ferry ride to Santoa. Discover hidden coves, take in breath-taking coastal vistas, and come across a variety of flora and fauna as you travel.

- **Gastronomy**: The fish and cuisine of Santander are well-known. Don't pass up the chance to savour delectable seafood delicacies like grilled clams, anchovies, and sardines. For a complete dining experience, serve your meal with a glass of sidra (cider) or local Cantabrian wine.

- Santander offers a beautiful fusion of scenic natural features, fascinating cultural landmarks, and an energetic seaside environment. Santander is certain to attract you with its beauty and variety of offerings, whether you're looking for leisure on the beach, discovering ancient buildings, or enjoying the local cuisine.

PRACTICAL INFORMATION

Here are some helpful hints when navigating Santander:

- Santander experiences warm marine weather, with chilly summers and mild winters. Winter temperatures typically range between 8°C and 14°C (46°F and 57°F), whereas summer temperatures typically range from 18°C to 25°C (64°F to 77°F). Before your vacation, it's a good idea to check the weather forecast and pack appropriately.

- Buses and taxis are also part of Santander's effective public transit system. Although it's simple to get around on foot in the city centre, buses are a practical way to get to other areas and tourist hotspots.

Taxis are easily accessible and may be either booked through taxi apps or hailed on the street.

- Santander Airport (SDR), which is about 5 kilometres (3 miles) west of the city centre, is the airport that serves Santander. Both internal and international flights are available, with links to important Spanish and European cities. You can take a taxi, bus, or rental car from the airport to get to the city's core.

- **Public transportation:** TUS is the firm in charge of running Santander's public bus system. Tickets for buses can be bought from the driver directly or through machines at bus stops. The buses travel a variety of routes throughout the city and its environs. You can also utilise the

"Tarjeta SIN," a reloadable transportation card, for convenience and financial savings.

- Santander provides a variety of lodging choices, including hotels, hostels, and rental homes. Due to their proximity to the beach and key attractions, the city centre and the Sardinero neighbourhood are popular places to stay. It's a good idea to reserve your lodging in advance, especially during the busiest travel season.

- The Euro (EUR) is Spain's official currency. Credit cards are often accepted in the majority of establishments, and ATMs are widely dispersed across the city. It is best to let your bank know about your trip intentions to prevent any problems with card usage.

- Spanish is the country's official language and is also used in Santander. In tourist hotspots, hotels, and larger institutions, English is spoken to some extent. It can be beneficial to learn a few fundamental Spanish phrases, particularly when communicating with natives.

- **Safety**: Santander is a reasonably safe city, but you should still exercise the usual caution. Watch out for pickpockets and keep a watch on your valuables, especially in crowded places. Additionally, it is advised to always use recognized taxis and to decline any trip offers made by strangers.
- Santander's shops and companies normally are open from Monday through Saturday, with the majority of them closing for a siesta break in the middle of the

day. Longer operating hours are frequently found in larger supermarkets and shopping complexes. Typically, restaurants open for lunch from 1:30 to 4:00 and dinner from 8:00 until midnight or later.
- **Information for travellers:** The Santander Tourist Office is situated in the heart of the city, next to Plaza Porticada. They offer details about trips, activities, and events in and around Santander. The staff can help you with any specific questions you may have as well as with maps and brochures.

Before your journey to Santander, be sure to check for any travel warnings or updates, and don't forget to take necessary items like a pair of comfortable walking shoes, sunscreen, and a travel adapter if necessary. Take your time and explore this lovely coastal city!

Transportation Within Bilbao

The main city in the Basque Country, Bilbao, has a number of practical means of transportation for travelling around.

- **Metro**: The effective Metro Bilbao system, which connects several areas of the city with Lines 1 and 2, is available in Bilbao. The metro is an easy and quick way to get from one neighbourhood to another and to popular destinations.

- Euskotren Tranbia, a contemporary tram network with three lines (A, E1, and E2), operates in Bilbao. The tram provides quick access to neighborhoods, commercial centres, and cultural attractions while covering important regions of the city.

- **Buses**: Bilbobus, the city's bus company, runs a vast bus network in Bilbao. Buses are a practical means of getting to places that the metro or tram does not go. The buses provide links to various neighbourhoods and attractions while also covering the city's centre and the nearby regions.

- Consider obtaining the Bilbao Bizkaia Card if you anticipate frequently using public transit. This card provides limitless access to the bus, tram, and metro systems in Bilbao and the surrounding area. Discounts on services and attractions are also offered.

- A public bike-sharing program named BilbaoBizi is available in Bilbao. Bicycles can be rented at a number of stations across the city and returned to any station when finished. It's a fantastic way to discover Bilbao's bike-friendly streets and picturesque places.

- **Taxis**: In Bilbao, you may easily hail a taxi on the street or locate one at a marked taxi stand. Taxis are a practical choice for getting to your location quickly, especially if you have a lot of luggage or want a more private ride.

- **Walking**: Bilbao is a city that is ideal for strolling, especially in the centre. There are many well-known sites, stores, and restaurants around that can be reached on foot. You can fully experience the city's colourful atmosphere and find hidden jewels while exploring it on foot.

- It's important to note that Bilbao's public transportation uses a contactless payment method. For your bus, metro, and tram fares, you can use a contactless card or a mobile payment system. Verify the timetables, frequency, and route maps for the specific transportation methods you intend to use.

Additionally, to efficiently plan your journeys and traverse the city's transit system, think about using navigation applications or reviewing local maps.

Accommodation Options

You can choose from a variety of lodging options in Bilbao to suit your interests and financial situation. Here are a few well-liked options:

- **Hotels**: Bilbao has a selection of hotels, ranging from high-end properties to more affordable ones. Both locally owned boutique hotels and well-known worldwide hotel chains are available. Since most hotels are found near the city's core, important attractions and transportation hubs are easily accessible.

- **Bed and Breakfasts and Guesthouses:** Bilbao is home to a number of wonderful bed and breakfasts and guesthouses. These smaller businesses frequently offer a more intimate and tailored experience, with warm accommodations and homey settings.

- **Apartments and Vacation Rentals:** Renting an apartment or vacation rental can be a fantastic alternative if you desire more room and the comfort of self-catering. You can select from a variety of sizes, locations, and facilities among the flats and holiday rentals offered by the different agencies and platforms in Bilbao.

- **Hostels**: Bilbao's hostels provide economical lodging options for tourists on a tight budget or seeking a more social setting. Hostels typically offer both private rooms and shared dormitory-style accommodations, and they frequently have social spaces where you may mingle with other visitors.

- **Paradores**: If you want a special and opulent experience, think about staying at a Parador. High-end hotels in Spain known as paradores are frequently found in picturesque or historic settings. Parador de Argómaniz, a parador in Bilbao, is roughly a one-hour drive from the city's centre.

- Think about things like location, accessibility to public transit, amenities, and previous guest evaluations when selecting your lodging. Booking your lodging in advance is advised, especially during busy travel times or when there are important events or festivals happening in Bilbao.

Additionally, if you participate in hotel loyalty programs or use online travel agencies, make sure to search for any discounts or deals that could help you cut the cost of your lodging.

Check the accommodations' check-in and check-out timings as well as any unique rules or regulations that may have been established.

Local Customs and Etiquette

Knowing the customs and etiquette of the city can help you have a polite and pleasurable trip to Bilbao. To remember, have the following in mind:

- A handshake is the traditional way to greet someone in Bilbao, both when you first meet them and in formal situations. Kisses on the cheek can be used to greet friends and strangers, beginning with the right cheek.

- Being on time is important in Bilbao. To be on time for meetings, appointments, or social events is considered polite. It is usual to let the person or group know if you expect to be late.

- **Dining Etiquette:** It is usual to wait until everyone is seated and the host gives the all-clear before beginning to eat when dining in Bilbao. Remember that dinner is frequently eaten later in the evening than in some other cultures, usually at or after 9:00 pm. It is polite to eat everything on your plate because it is often frowned upon to waste food.

- Bilbao has a very relaxed dress code compared to other cities. However, it's always advisable to present yourself cleanly and respectfully while going to formal gatherings, religious locations, or luxury restaurants. Smart-casual clothes are typically suitable in environments that are more relaxed, such as restaurants or bars.

- Spanish is the official language in Bilbao. Even though many residents, especially in tourist regions, understand English, it's a good idea to acquire a few fundamental Spanish words and phrases to communicate more effectively. Any effort to speak their language is appreciated by the locals.

- **Tipping**: In Bilbao, tipping is less typical or anticipated than in some other places. A tiny gratuity is still appreciated for good service, though. In restaurants, it's customary to round up the check or, if you're extremely happy with the service, give a 5–10% gratuity.

- **Respect for Basque Culture**: Bilbao is located in the centre of Basque Country, where the traditions and culture are very important. Respect the Basque people's culture by being understanding and appreciative of their traditions. Learn about Basque history, music, and food to better comprehend the way of life there.

- **Public Conduct:** It's crucial to exercise consideration for others and keep noise levels down when in public areas. In places that are supposed to be peaceful, like museums, libraries, or public transit, refrain from loud talks or disruptive behaviour.

You can establish friendly relationships with people and demonstrate your respect for Bilbao and the Basque Country's culture and traditions by adhering to these traditions and using common politeness.

Safety Tips and Emergency Contacts

Prioritise your safety when visiting Bilbao, and be ready for any unforeseen circumstances. Here are some safety recommendations to bear in mind and contact information for emergencies:

- Be aware of your surroundings and exercise caution, especially in congested places or popular tourist destinations.
- Be wary of pickpockets and secure your possessions. Put your belongings in a safe bag or money belt.
- Use crowded, well-lit streets, especially late at night.
- When crossing roadways, observe the laws of the road.
- Never show off enormous sums of money or expensive objects in public.

- Respect regional traditions and follow any safety instructions or cautions issued by authorities.

Numbers for emergencies
- Emergency General: 112
- Officers: 092
- Emergency Medical Care: 112 or 061
- 080 Fire Department

- **Language Barrier:** Learning a few fundamental Spanish words will help you ask for aid or communicate in an emergency. For a list of basic Spanish phrases, go to the earlier response on this page.

Local laws and ordinances
- To make sure you adhere to the law, familiarise yourself with the Basque Country and Bilbao's local laws and ordinances.

- Be aware of any special rules governing how people should act in public, how they should consume alcohol, and how they should smoke.
- **Health and travel insurance**: It is advised to have all-inclusive travel insurance that protects you against medical costs, mishaps, and other unforeseen events while you are away.
- Have a copy of your prescriptions or any relevant medical records on hand and carry any essential prescription drugs.
- Weather and Natural Disasters: Be aware of the weather and any possible natural disasters that might happen while you're there.
- Follow the guidance of the local authorities, take cover, and, if necessary, evacuate.

Keep in mind that these pointers are merely general recommendations, and it's crucial to keep up with the latest safety updates in Bilbao while you're there. Observe any advice or suggestions made by local authorities. You may have a safe and fun day touring Bilbao by being cautious, well-prepared, and considerate.

Useful Websites and Resources

It's beneficial to have access to trustworthy websites and sources that offer current advice and information when arranging a vacation to Bilbao. To help you, the following websites and resources are listed:

- Bilbao's official tourism website, www.bilbao turismo.net, provides a plethora of information on the city, including details on its attractions, events, lodging options, culinary establishments, and transportation.

- **Bilbao City Council**: Details on the city's services, news, and events can be found on the council's website (www.bilbao.eus). It's a helpful tool to keep up with local events while you're there.

- **Lonely Planet**: Renowned travel guide publisher Lonely Planet (www.lonelyplanet.com) provides a thorough guidebook on Bilbao that includes in-depth details on attractions, restaurants, lodging, and suggested itineraries.

- TripAdvisor is a well-known travel site where you can read reviews, rate lodgings, restaurants, and attractions in Bilbao, as well as get recommendations from other travellers. It can be a useful tool for getting information and making wise choices.

- **Bilbao Now:** Bilbao Now is an online magazine that offers news on the most recent events, festivals, exhibitions, and cultural activities in the city (www.bilbaonow.com). It's a fantastic tool for learning about Bilbao's vibrant cultural scene.

- **Tourism in the Basque Country:** The Tourism in the Basque Country website (www.euskoguide.com) provides information on attractions throughout the Basque Country in addition to Bilbao. It offers information about the regional culture, landmarks, and activities.

- **Transport Services:** Websites like the official airport website (www.aena.es) and the public transportation website (www.ctb.eus) of Bilbao offer details on ways to get around the city and to/from the airport.

- Checking the weather forecast is important while making outdoor activity plans. Reliable weather data for Bilbao can be found on websites like AccuWeather's (www.accuweather.com) or HAEMET (www.aemet.es), Spain's national weather service.

To ensure you have access to the most current and correct information, visit the official websites and resources. These tools will help you get the most out of your vacation to Bilbao and make sure everything goes smoothly.

LANGUAGE GUIDE

Having a working knowledge of the local tongue will greatly improve your trip to Bilbao. Although English is widely spoken by locals in Bilbao, it is always appreciated to try to communicate in Spanish. Spanish is the city's official language. Here is a language guide with some words and phrases you might find helpful:

Greetings:
- Hello: Hola
- Good morning: Buenos días
- Good afternoon/evening: Buenas tardes
- Good night: Buenas noches
- How are you?: ¿Cómo estás? (informal) / ¿Cómo está usted? (formal)

Basic Expressions:
- Yes: Sí

- No: No
- Please: Por favor
- Thank you: Gracias
- You're welcome: De nada
- Excuse me: Disculpe / Perdón
- I'm sorry: Lo siento

Introductions:
- My name is...: Me llamo...
- What is your name?: ¿Cómo te llamas? (informal) / ¿Cómo se llama usted? (formal)
- Nice to meet you: Mucho gusto

Asking for Help:
- Can you help me, please?: ¿Me puede ayudar, por favor?
- I don't understand: No entiendo
- Could you repeat that, please?: ¿Puede repetir eso, por favor?
- Where is...?: ¿Dónde está...?

Ordering Food and Drinks:
- I would like...: Me gustaría...

- What do you recommend?: ¿Qué me recomienda?
- The bill, please: La cuenta, por favor
- Cheers!: ¡Salud!

Directions:
- Where is the...?: ¿Dónde está el/la...?
- Left: Izquierda
- Right: Derecha
- Straight ahead: Todo recto
- Excuse me, where is the nearest metro station?: Disculpe, ¿dónde está la estación de metro más cercana?

Numbers:
- 1: uno
- 2: dos
- 3: tres
- 4: cuatro
- 5: cinco
- 10: diez

- 20: veinte
- 100: cien

Keep in mind to talk slowly and clearly, particularly if your Spanish is not very good. Locals will likely be more understanding and helpful if you try to speak to them in their language.

Additionally useful are smartphone translation apps or a pocket-sized Spanish-English dictionary for rapid reference.

Your journey to Bilbao may be made more enjoyable and rewarding by learning your native tongue. Even if your pronunciation isn't great, don't be scared to try out a few sentences. The majority of the time, the locals will be appreciative of your efforts and may even volunteer to assist you in honing your Spanish.

Basic Spanish Phrases

Certainly! The following fundamental Spanish words and phrases can come in handy while you visit Bilbao:

Greetings and Basics:
- Hello: Hola
- Goodbye: Adiós
- Yes: Sí
- No: No
- Please: Por favor
- Thank you: Gracias
- You're welcome: De nada
- Excuse me: Disculpe
- I'm sorry: Lo siento
- How are you?: ¿Cómo estás? (informal) / ¿Cómo está usted? (formal)
- I don't understand: No entiendo

Introductions:

- My name is...: Me llamo...
- What is your name?: ¿Cómo te llamas? (informal) / ¿Cómo se llama usted? (formal)
- Nice to meet you: Mucho gusto

Directions:
- Where is...?: ¿Dónde está...?
- Left: Izquierda
- Right: Derecha
- Straight ahead: Todo recto
- Excuse me, where is the nearest...?: Disculpe, ¿dónde está el/la más cercano/a...?

Ordering Food and Drinks:
- I would like...: Me gustaría...
- What do you recommend?: ¿Qué me recomienda?
- The bill, please: La cuenta, por favor
- Do you have a menu in English?: ¿Tienen un menú en inglés?

- A table for two, please: Una mesa para dos, por favor

Shopping:
- How much does it cost?: ¿Cuánto cuesta?
- I'm just looking: Sólo estoy mirando
- Do you have this in a different colour/size?: ¿Tiene esto en otro colour/talla?

Transportation:
- Where is the nearest bus/metro station?: ¿Dónde está la estación de autobuses/metro más cercana?
- How much is a ticket to...?: ¿Cuánto cuesta un boleto para...?
- When does the next train/bus leave?: ¿Cuándo sale el próximo tren/autobús?

Emergency:
- Help!: ¡Ayuda!

- I need a doctor: Necesito un médico
- Where 's the nearest hospital?: ¿Dónde está el hospital más cercano?

Remember that knowing these words and phrases will help you a lot when you are in Bilbao, as will having a basic grasp of the language. Don't be frightened to try; the people there will appreciate your attempt to speak their language.

CONCLUSION

For those who are considering visiting Bilbao, "Travel Guide to Bilbao 2023: Exploring the Vibrant City" is a thorough guide that offers helpful advice. This guide covers every facet of discovering the bustling city, from helpful hints and crucial travel information to in-depth insights on neighbourhoods, attractions, eating, and day trips.

This guide will assist you in navigating the city and maximising your time there, whether your interests are in Bilbao's extensive history and culture, gorgeous architecture, top-notch museums, mouthwatering Basque food, or exciting nightlife.

This book attempts to improve your experience by offering insightful information on regional cultures, attractions, and hidden jewels through thorough descriptions, useful recommendations, and insider advice. It gives you a well-rounded view of the city and allows you to fully experience Bilbao's distinctive ambiance while making lifelong memories.

Pack your luggage, grab our travel guide, and get ready to travel to Bilbao, where you'll find the ideal fusion of culture, cuisine, art, and spectacular natural beauty. Make the most of your stay in Bilbao by enjoying your experience in this energetic city!

Fond Farewell to Bilbao

It's time to say a fond farewell to the colourful city that has won your heart as your time in Bilbao draws to a close. Take a minute to appreciate everything Bilbao has to offer you as you think back on the memories you've built and the experiences you've had.

- Bid adieu to the Old Town's (Casco Viejo) lovely streets, where you walked through its winding lanes and took in the atmosphere of the past. Say goodbye to the Guggenheim Museum, a modern architectural wonder whose eye-catching design and engaging exhibits left you in amazement.

- Take one more stroll along the Nervion River's banks, remembering the beauty all about you as you admire the magnificent

Zubizuri Bridge. Enjoy some more pintxos and a drink of Txakoli wine while savouring the tastes of Basque cuisine.

- Appreciate the sincere connections you've made along the trip and express gratitude to the people for their warm welcome. Keep in mind the warm exchanges of words, smiles, and memories that helped to make your trip in Bilbao so memorable.

- Carry the dynamic energy of the city and the experiences that will last a lifetime with you as you depart Bilbao. Keep in mind the sights, sounds, and flavours of this extraordinary location, and use them to motivate your future adventures.

Hello, Bilbao! May your cultural scene flourish till we meet again, and may your natural beauty continue to enthral those who come to see it. Thank you Bilbao for a wonderful time..

Printed in Great Britain
by Amazon